THESE ARE
THE DAYS OF
ELIJAH

How God Uses Ordinary People
to Do Extraordinary Things

R. T. KENDALL

Chosen
a division of Baker Publishing Group
Minneapolis, Minnesota

© 2013 by R. T. Kendall

Published by Chosen Books
11400 Hampshire Avenue South
Bloomington, Minnesota 55438
www.chosenbooks.com

Chosen Books is a division of
Baker Publishing Group, Grand Rapids, Michigan

Printed in the United States of America

Library of Congress Cataloging-in-Publication Data
Kendall, R. T.
    These are the days of Elijah : how God uses ordinary people to do
extraordinary things / R. T. Kendall.
        pages cm
    Summary: "Beloved Bible teacher explores the life of the greatest prophet,
showing how God regularly uses ordinary, everyday people to accomplish
extraordinary things. Accessible but comprehensive"—Provided by publisher.
    ISBN 978-0-8007-9537-5 (pbk. : alk. paper)
    1. Elijah (Biblical prophet) I. Title.
BS580.E4K53 2013
222'.5092—dc23   2012042338

The internet addresses, email addresses, and phone numbers in this book are accurate at the time of publication. They are provided as a resource. Baker Publishing Group does not endorse them or vouch for their content or permanence.

Cover design by Franke Design and Illustration

18 19 20 21 22 23 24   11 10 9 8 7 6 5

"Who better to unfold the dynamism, impact, character and lifetime of one of the greatest biblical prophets than one of this century's wisest and most insightful commentators?"

Robin Mark, award-winning musician and composer of "Days of Elijah"

"This is a book that every prophetically gifted person should read."

John Paul Jackson, founder and president, Streams Ministries International

"It seems every book R. T. Kendall writes becomes my 'new favorite.' That's because he always has a fresh, life-giving word for the people of God. His latest work on Elijah is an excellent case in point. In an age of cynicism and hopelessness, R. T. reminds us that God never abandons His people or His Kingdom plan."

Stephen Chitty, senior pastor, Christian Life Assembly, Columbia, South Carolina

"R. T. has been a friend and mentor to me for the past several years. His books and messages have shaped my life in profound ways. As I read this book on the life of Elijah, I was encouraged and challenged with the reality that Elijah was a man just like me. Yet he lived life with a deep faith—a faith with which I, too, can live."

David McQueen, senior pastor, Beltway Park Baptist Church, Abilene, Texas

"This book highlights the importance of godly character as well as it unveils the 'ways of God.' We don't hear about teaching on this subject enough, but it is of necessity that these truths are being spoken about and taught in these days! Godly gifting must coincide with godly character, and I was amazed at the insight this book brings out in both! I highly recommend this book!"

Jeff Dollar, senior pastor, Grace Center, Franklin, Tennessee

Contents

CONTENTS

Foreword

Abraham Heschel once wrote, "To be a prophet is both a distinction and an affliction." Elijah was no exception. Few prophets in Scripture have provoked as many ministers, challenged as many evangelists and inspired as many prophets as Elijah. This man from the desert, who seemed to be on the one hand invincible and on the other hand cowardly, was as much an enigma then as he is today.

He is unique. He could run faster than a horse-driven chariot. He is one of two humans in Scripture taken to heaven before they tasted death. He is the only one, other than Jesus, who, it is prophesied, will return to earth before the "Day of the Lord." He is one of two who have seen the backside of God as He passed by. If that is not strange enough, he is the only one with an anointing great enough to call down fire from heaven. He was in the lineage of the ecstatic prophets, whose mere presence seemed to defy human anticipation, and to be determined solely by the Spirit of God rather than themselves.

Yet Elijah was also human, with emotions, fears, doubts and moments of elation, just like you and me. He lived in an era of high occult activity. He was a focal point in the clash between Yahweh and Baal, spurred on by Ahab, who sold himself to do evil, and even more so by Jezebel, who would stop at nothing, including murdering the innocent and worshiping demons, to get her way. Elijah stood up against the odds and proclaimed Mosaic righteousness when decadence was politically correct.

Elijah was a paradox, a walking contradiction of foresight and blindness, faith and fear, power and weakness. He killed 850 false prophets, yet ran from one woman. He demanded that a dying widow feed him before she fed herself and her son, then years later raised that son from the dead. Egocentrically he complained to God that he alone was left, and God had to burst that bubble by telling him there were seven thousand others who had not bowed their knees to Baal. He complained of hunger, ate food brought to him by ravens and walked two hundred miles to Mount Sinai after eating one loaf of bread that an angel baked for him.

Elijah taunted kings, complained to God, healed people and actually changed the course of nature. Elijah was a prophet's prophet, a man's man with a nature just like yours and mine.

R. T. Kendall has captured a stable of hidden truths that lie behind the scenes in the life of this unique prophet and man of God. He unfolds how God took a weak man and transformed him into a giant. He discloses the importance of the overlooked, and he rightly positions God as the core of Elijah's life. R. T.'s insight and biblical knowledge allow him to clarify the levels in which God speaks to and through prophets. That alone is worth a hundred times the price of this book.

R. T. has also unraveled the mystery of what I feel is the oft-overlooked crux of Elijah's ministry: He was a human being who dared to believe God would use him. That is not as simple as the novice might think. In *These Are the Days of Elijah*, R. T. Kendall has found a way of making the complex seem simple. He has untangled the knot that others have tried to untie and could not.

Every pastor, evangelist and teacher should read this book; and it is a "must-read" for all who believe they might have even a small modicum of prophetic gifting.

John Paul Jackson
Founder, Streams Ministries International

Introduction

Elijah was one of the most outstanding prophets of the Old Testament—and certainly the most colorful. He stands next to Moses, the greatest prophet of all. It was Moses and Elijah who appeared on the Mount of Transfiguration with Jesus (see Matthew 17:3). These two men represented the Law (Moses) and the prophets (Elijah) of the Old Testament.

Elijah was in the succession of a new era of prophets beginning with Samuel. Between the time of Moses and Samuel the word of God was "rare," which means that God had not raised up many to speak His word for a long period of time (see 1 Samuel 3:1). But with the emergence of Samuel a new kind of prophetic ministry was begun, anticipating men like Nathan (see 2 Samuel 7:2), Gad (see 2 Samuel 24:11) and Elijah—and eventually the canonical prophets like Isaiah and Jeremiah whose words became Scripture.

Elijah was not a canonical prophet (there is no book in the Bible named after him), but his ministry and impact were unforgettable. Although his successor Elisha is said to have had double the anointing that was on Elijah (see 2 Kings 2:9–12), future generations remembered Elijah more than they did Elisha. He was mentioned at the end of the book of Malachi (see Malachi 4:5–6). Gabriel said that John the Baptist would go before the Lord in the spirit and power of Elijah (see Luke 1:17). When Jesus cried out in Aramaic, "*Eloi, Eloi, lama sabachthani*," bystanders thought He was calling for Elijah (see Mark 15:34–35).

Prophets were known as "seers" through the time of Samuel (see 1 Samuel 9:9). An example of the gifting of seer was Samuel's discerning that Saul (before he was king) was trying to find some lost donkeys. Looking for the seer, they came upon Samuel who acknowledged his position and then added—before being told why he was being sought—"As for the donkeys you lost three days ago, do not worry about them; they have been found" (1 Samuel 9:20).

The role of the prophet was expanded to include not only seeing into people's lives but also speaking directly for God—and even predicting the future. The canonical prophets predicted not only the immediate future but sometimes the far distant future, as in the case of people like Isaiah and Daniel. Elijah's time of ministry was in between the era of early prophets and canonical prophets. He was a man who confronted idolatry in Israel but also who performed miracles.

What strikes me most about Elijah is that he was both extraordinary and ordinary. He was spectacular—stating boldly, for example, that it would not rain until he gave the word; and there was not a drop of rain for three and a half years. Yet James noted that Elijah was a man "just like us" because he was so very, very human (James 5:17). Elijah took himself too seriously; he felt he was the only prophet around who was worth a grain of salt and fancied he was a cut above all before him. He was very human indeed. This is what makes a study of Elijah so thrilling. If God could use a man as human as Elijah was, there is hope for all of us!

My first recollection of the name *Elijah* goes back to my childhood memories. My first pastor, the Rev. Gene Phillips, preached a sermon on Elijah in my old church in Ashland, Kentucky. I was probably eight years old. I do not remember a single word in the sermon, but I remember the atmosphere. The impact was electric. My father reckoned it was the greatest sermon he ever heard. What a wonderful gift that a preacher could be remembered like that, and yet Elijah's very life and ministry would be remembered forever!

The following chapters are edited from my final series of Sunday evening sermons I preached as minister of Westminster Chapel, from September 2000 to December 2001. I pray that each of these will be used by the Holy Spirit to speak directly to your heart and life.

1

The Oath

> Now Elijah the Tishbite, from Tishbe in Gilead,
> said to Ahab, "As the LORD, the God of Israel, lives,
> whom I serve, there will be neither dew nor rain
> in the next few years except at my word."
>
> 1 Kings 17:1

Without any introduction, warning, explanation or preparation for what was coming, Elijah suddenly appears. Out of the blue. Just like that. He is simply called Elijah the Tishbite. We are not given any more information except that he was from Gilead and that he made a stunning prediction to Ahab the king who had done "more evil in the eyes of the LORD" than any of the kings before him (1 Kings 16:30).

Elijah confronted the wicked Ahab with an amazing word—that there would not be a drop of rain, not even dew on the grass, unless Elijah himself commanded it. "Except at my word," said Elijah. Extraordinary. Bold. You could almost say it was an impudent, if not immodest, claim. "I alone will determine when it will rain next," Elijah was shamelessly predicting. Not since the days of Moses had there been anyone like him.

The Atmosphere in His Day

The times in which Elijah flourished were characterized by an atmosphere of spiritual degeneration. This was during the era of the wicked King Ahab. Ahab not only considered it "trivial to commit the sins of Jeroboam," but married Jezebel—an evil woman—and began to serve and worship Baal. Ahab did more to provoke the Lord "than did all the kings of Israel before him" (1 Kings 16:31–33).

It was a demonic atmosphere in which Elijah ministered. *Baal* means "lord, master, owner, possessor." To worship Baal was to open one's heart to the demonic world. Every Christian needs to learn not to play fast and loose with the demonic—such as playing with a Ouija board, following your astrology chart or going to a fortune-teller. Avoid these with all your heart. In the case of Ahab, there was more, for he rebuilt Jericho and did so in the face of Joshua's pronouncement generations before: "Cursed before the LORD is the man who undertakes to rebuild this city, Jericho" (Joshua 6:26).

How would you like to live in an atmosphere like that? Many ministers today look for a church that is already established or want to preach where there are many Christians. They want to be in a Bible belt. Elijah did not have that privilege. God looks for people who will go outside their comfort zones. Part of the genius of the apostle Paul, for example, was that he wanted to go where the Gospel had not been known (see Romans 15:20). I am reminded of something John Wesley wrote in his journal when he observed the evil and wickedness in Newcastle, England: "Never in my life have I heard such language, such swearing and have seen such wickedness. Ripe for revival."

I think you and I are in an evil day, too. We *could* run away from our responsibilities or make excuses for the conditions of our time. Or we could adopt Wesley's position and see things as being a good sign that God might step in soon! After all, God sent Jesus into the world when conditions in Israel were at their worst. This is why He died on a cross. Paul could say, "Where sin increased, grace increased all the more" (Romans 5:20).

The name *Elijah* means "my God is Yahweh." In the Old Testament a person's name was often bound up with his calling. He had a nickname: Elijah "the Tishbite, from Tishbe in Gilead." Gilead was an area east of the Jordan River in Manasseh. *Tishbe* also means "settler," but little else is known.

Elijah was almost certainly a lonely man. Many of God's sovereign vessels are very lonely, including those who are married. I predict that when we get to heaven we will be amazed how many of God's choice servants were unhappily married—as in the case of both George Whitefield and John Wesley. But sometimes lonely people—partly because they are not always accountable to anybody—take themselves too seriously. It was certainly one of Elijah's weaknesses.

Although we know little about the man Elijah before his appearance in 1 Kings 17:1, his opening statement to Ahab tells a lot about his relationship to the God of Israel. He revealed several important things to Ahab in this opening line—such as the nature of God and God's commitment to the people He has chosen. Here are five particular points he made.

The Living God

First, Elijah showed something of the nature of his God. Elijah's God is the *living* God. He not only exists but is alive and active. His God is not what deists would call an "absentee watchmaker"—a God who made the world and left it to run on its own. No. Elijah's God is totally on top of things, in constant touch day and night with all His people and all creation. As the old spiritual put it, "He sees all we do, He hears all we say." Nothing escapes God's notice and everything that is going on matters deeply to Him. But that was not Elijah's main point here in confronting Ahab.

There is a type of evangelical today known as "cessationist." This means that God "ceased" to deal with His people in an extraordinary manner after the closing of the canon of Scripture. Before the canon of Scripture was complete, there were signs, wonders and miracles, but they ended once the canon was complete. From that time on God speaks only through His Word—the Bible.

The trouble with this point of view is that it is not warranted in Scripture at all, but is a conclusion some good and sincere theologians have drawn owing to the apparent absence of signs and wonders in the Church. Some people have hastily, but permanently, dug their heels in and have refused to acknowledge any extraordinary work of God today as authentic—since God does not do this anymore! It is quite sad. They are truly deists in evangelical dress.

The canon of Scripture is indeed closed. Nothing can be added to it. It does not follow, however, that God cannot do miraculous things today. God enabled Elijah to speak at *oath level* although he was not a canonical prophet. What does it mean to speak at oath level? Briefly it means to speak with assurance that you have it right; it is God's final word on the subject. We will explore this at some length at the end of this chapter. There is no reason God cannot speak through someone like that today. It does not mean for a second that one is adding to Scripture. Indeed, such power and authority would extol and honor Scripture more than ever. It would demonstrate that God is indeed the *living* God.

Elijah's main point here was that his word to Ahab was as reliable as the very existence of God. Elijah's word was literally as dependable as God Himself. "If God lives, then my word is true," Elijah was saying. "If there is a God, it's not going to rain." To put it conversely, Elijah was virtually saying, "If it rains, there is no God." In other words, as surely as there is a God, one can forget about rain until Elijah gave permission for it to rain.

The God of Israel

Second, Elijah's God is connected with a people and a nation: Israel. God in His sovereign purpose chose Israel to be His people. "For you are a people holy to the LORD your God. The LORD your God has chosen you out of all the peoples on the face of the earth to be his people, his treasured possession" (Deuteronomy 7:6). He chose Israel not because they were more numerous, for they were "the fewest of all peoples. But it was because the LORD loved you and kept the oath he swore to your forefathers" (Deuteronomy 7:7–8). As it is written, "I will have mercy on whom I will have mercy, and I will have compassion on whom I will have compassion" (Exodus 33:19; see also Romans 9:14).

Elijah, therefore, spoke for the *God of Israel* and addressed Ahab who was a king in Israel but who had forgotten God's covenant and ways. Ahab was in a most precarious state and yet was privileged—even if he was ungrateful—to have a true word of God addressed to him.

God's Trust in Elijah

Third, the fact that God would allow Elijah to speak to Ahab on oath-level authority shows God's trust in this prophet. I cannot imagine a greater privilege on this planet than to speak directly for God in this fashion. This is truly to be entrusted with a "thus says the Lord."

Frankly, I do not think God grants this every day. I personally think it is extremely rare, as it was even in Elijah's day. It is not the same thing as expository teaching—as I am doing in writing this book. I am, therefore, not claiming to speak at oath level. Sorry if this disappoints you! One of my editors told me that he had a writer who would not allow his material to be edited. "Every word I write is from God," the man actually claimed, and would not allow an editor to mess with his stuff! This is silly. Only a canonical writer speaks with infallibility. God *may* grant a sovereign vessel to speak at oath level, but such a person should always be open to criticism and scrutiny.

That said, I hope, as I write, that I am truly speaking for God and believe I am indeed doing this—but only to the degree I am being *faithful to the true meaning* of His Word. God is the judge of that. But to be given oath-level authority is to have the infallible, verbal command of the Spirit whereby one *knows* he is saying exactly what God wants said. Elijah had precisely that at times, as when he told Ahab it would not rain. But he did not always have it! We will see below that this extraordinary prophet could get "in the flesh" and say things that would make the angels blush. In any case, to speak with the authority of God's oath was an inestimable honor and privilege.

Elijah's Allegiance

Fourth, notice the words *whom I serve*. That lets Ahab know immediately whose side Elijah was on and where he was coming from. Elijah's sole allegiance was to the God of Israel. He *served* the God of Israel. He did what God said "Do," went where God said "Go" and said what God said "Say." This means that Elijah could not be bribed or persuaded to do anything or say anything but what God Himself commanded him to say or do.

The Church needs more people like that around today. Too many people have a "price"; that is, if the bid is high enough, they can be persuaded to compromise, alter their messages or leave out what might be offensive. It might come not merely with the promise of money, but perhaps with the promise of position, a promise of whom they can meet and be seen with or a promise of some favor coming down the road. It is unthinkable that the Elijahs, the John the Baptists and the apostle Pauls of this world could be tempted successfully to change their messages to suit their hearers. Paul himself said that in the last days there would be a "great number of teachers to say what their itching ears want to hear" (2 Timothy 4:3).

The Oath: Infallibility

Finally—and most importantly—contained in Elijah's word to Ahab is a phenomenon we must try further to understand before we move on in this book. It is a much neglected teaching, but one that is thrilling and rewarding to the person who grasps it: the meaning and place of the oath. As we have seen, Elijah confronted Ahab with an oath: "As the Lord, the God of Israel, lives." This is "oath language." (See Jeremiah 5:2, where the exact phrase is used in conjunction with an oath.)

In a word, *oath* means "infallibility." It may be applied several ways. It can refer, for example, to the assurance of salvation, which the Westminster Confession declares to be "infallible assurance." It can refer to advanced knowledge that your prayer will be answered, knowing that your prayer is "heard" (see 1 John 5:14–15). It is supernatural knowledge imparted by the Holy Spirit.

The promise and oath are "two unchangeable things," according to Hebrews 6:18, in which it is "impossible for God to lie," but the oath is stronger. Sometimes God makes a promise; less frequently He swears an oath. Is there a difference? Yes. Whereas both are *equally true*, the promise is usually conditional. An "if" is often indicated. "*If* my people, who are called by my name, will humble themselves and pray and seek my face and turn from their wicked ways, *then* will I hear from heaven and will forgive their sin and will heal their land" (2 Chronicles 7:14, emphasis added). This is a *promise* from God. It is absolutely true but is conditional: *If . . . then.*

Sometimes the "if" is not explicit but implied. Take John 3:16, the Bible in a nutshell: "For God so loved the world that he gave his one and only Son, that whoever believes in him shall not perish but have eternal life." This is perhaps the best known promise in the Bible—the promise of eternal life. There is no "if" in John 3:16, but it is implied: Only those who believe shall have eternal life.

The oath, however, is typically carried out without any conditions; when God swears an oath, nothing can stop it from being fulfilled. "I declared on oath in my anger, 'They shall never enter my rest'" (Hebrews 3:11). Although the children of Israel tried to enter Canaan, after God swore in His wrath they failed to do so (see Numbers 14:44–45). In other words, once God has sworn an oath, there is nothing anyone can do to change His mind.

The swearing of the oath by God may be directed by Him in two ways: in wrath or in mercy. God swore in His wrath that Israel would not get their inheritance, and that generation indeed died in the wilderness (see Hebrews 3:17–19). God swore in His mercy to Abraham: "I swear by myself, declares the LORD, that because you have done this and have not withheld your son, your only son . . ." (Genesis 22:16). The result was that Abraham's seed would be as innumerable as the grains of sand on the seashore and the stars in the heavens.

Initially, from Genesis 12:1 to Genesis 22, God spoke to Abraham by *promise*. God promised Abraham that his seed would be as the stars in the heavens. Abraham believed the promise and was regarded righteous by his faith (see Genesis 15:6). The promise was repeated after that until we get to Genesis 22:16, when the promise was upgraded: God now swore an *oath* to Abraham. Hebrews 6:13 notes that God "swore by himself" to Abraham because He could swear by no greater. This is because people always swear "by someone greater" (Hebrews 6:16). They do this to convince others that they are absolutely telling the truth. I have heard people say, "I swear by my mother's grave," in order to prove they are telling the truth or will keep their promise. The president of the United States generally takes the oath of office on the

Bible. The oath signifies absolute assurance that the truth is being told and the promise will be kept.

Elijah swore *by God* when he went before King Ahab and pronounced on oath: "As the LORD, the God of Israel, lives, whom I serve, there will be neither dew nor rain in the next few years except at my word" (1 Kings 17:1). This was a word that could not be changed, even if the whole nation of Israel fasted and prayed for many days. Elijah did not bite his nails for the next three years, worrying that it might rain and thereby destroy his prophetic reputation. When God grants the oath all doubting disappears.

Or to quote Hebrews, the oath "puts an end to all argument" (Hebrews 6:16). It appeals to the highest authority—God Himself. One should be extremely cautious, therefore, when speaking directly for God. I am afraid there are a lot of would-be prophets around who carelessly claim "God told me" and have no idea what they are doing or saying. Elijah, however, had *truly* heard from God and knew what he was doing.

When Elijah confronted Ahab with the words *As the Lord, the God of Israel lives*, he was informing the wicked king that God Himself was at the bottom of this prophecy that there would be no rain. It was not really Elijah's word at all; it was an infallible, direct and immediate word from God. Elijah was merely the instrument, the vehicle, that conveyed this word.

This man Elijah, who stepped in out of the blue, spoke with a level of authority that seldom appears on the earth. Only people like Moses and Samuel had spoken like this before. That is the way the life and ministry of Elijah is introduced. We now proceed to examine this extraordinary, but ordinary, man.

2

Knowing the Next Step Forward

> Then the word of the LORD came to Elijah: "Leave here, turn eastward and hide in the Kerith Ravine, east of the Jordan. You will drink from the brook, and I have ordered the ravens to feed you there." So he did what the LORD had told him. He went to the Kerith Ravine, east of the Jordan, and stayed there. The ravens brought him bread and meat in the morning and bread and meat in the evening, and he drank from the brook.
>
> 1 Kings 17:2–6

The Holy Spirit always knows the next thing we should do, the next step forward. Elijah needed wisdom to know what to do now that he had confronted King Ahab. *Wisdom* may be defined as "the presence of the mind of the Holy Spirit."

We learn later that Ahab looked high and low over Israel to find Elijah. As David spent twenty years running from King Saul to stay alive, so, too, Elijah was on the run. It was part of his being prepared for future ministry.

To be entrusted with oath-level assurance of God's will is arguably the greatest honor and privilege that a human being can receive. It is an infallible knowledge that God occasionally gives to His chosen servants. That is what happened to Elijah when he could categorically and authoritatively tell King Ahab that it would not rain unless he said so. But, at the same time, the person to whom such assurance is given is still human. I think it would be hard *not* to take oneself quite seriously, having been entrusted with such insight. We will see throughout this book that Elijah did indeed take himself very seriously. What is thrilling is how patient God was with Elijah. God knows our frame and remembers that we are "dust" (Psalm 103:14).

There was no natural explanation for what Elijah was able to convey to Ahab. Not that Ahab believed Elijah! The evil king was so filled with unbelief and the demonic that Elijah's word was, in a sense, wasted. What also was happening—which the account in 1 Kings makes no mention of—is that Elijah not only prophesied but *prayed*. It is James who tells us that Elijah "prayed earnestly that it would not rain" (James 5:17). The prayer no doubt preceded Elijah's solemn declaration to Ahab. You may ask, Was it God's idea or Elijah's that it would not rain? It was both, but the idea began with God. God put the thought in Elijah's heart. Elijah then asked God that it would not rain—as though it was entirely Elijah's idea. But he would not have known to make such a request had not God put it in his heart.

We saw above that one of the ways the oath may be applied is by having advance knowledge that one's prayer will be answered. John said, "If *we know that he hears us*—whatever we ask—*we know that we have* what we asked of him" (1 John 5:15, emphasis added). Elijah *knew that he was heard*; he went, therefore, to Ahab with the absolute knowledge that what he prophesied would come to pass.

Preparation

It may surprise you when I say that this kind of authority and power meant that Elijah would need further preparation. This is one of the great paradoxes of the Christian life: We need more and more preparation when we have more and more of the Holy Spirit. One might think that if we are full of the Holy Spirit, surely that is all the preparation we need. Wrong! We need preparation more than ever! It is partly because of the human tendency in all of us to take ourselves too seriously when we are given more and more success.

When Samuel anointed David to be king, "from that day on the Spirit of the LORD came upon David in power" (1 Samuel 16:13). But it would be another twenty years before David would be king. Why? It is because—strange as it may seem—being Spirit-filled is not enough. David's anointing would need to be *refined*. He was only seventeen years old. He was not ready to be king!

It takes a lot of maturity to admit to the need of preparation. Age helps us to come to our senses. Charles Spurgeon, one of the greatest preachers of all time, said that if he knew he had 25 years left to live he would spend twenty of them in preparation. Billy Graham said much the same thing, that if he had his life to live over, he would spend more time in preparation.

But God also has a way of doing on-the-job preparation. He did this with Elijah. Elijah's greatest work lay in the future, when one day he would confront the false prophets of Baal. This would take place while the famine was still on, before the rain came—when Ahab had no choice but to listen to Elijah. Three years without rain got Ahab's attention.

The three years after Elijah's edict to Ahab were the era of preparation for Elijah. Those years were as vital to Elijah's development as they were crucial for bringing Ahab to openness regarding Elijah.

Are you in preparation? Perhaps you are Spirit-filled. Could it be that you are not ready—even yet—for the greatest job God has in mind for you? Whom the Lord loves He chastens—disciplines—and He "punishes everyone he accepts as a son" (Hebrews 12:6). This punishment is not a case of God "getting even" with us owing to some terrible sin in our past. No, it is God getting us ready for what is coming. Chastening is essentially preparation. It enables us to share in God's holiness (see Hebrews 12:10), thus producing "a harvest of righteousness and peace for those who have been trained by it" (verse 11). The more God uses you, the more you will need preparation. I can tell you candidly, at the age of 76 I am still being prepared.

Elijah needed more preparation. After he left the presence of Israel's king, he was ordered to turn eastward and hide in the Kerith Ravine where he would drink from the brook and be fed by the ravens. I have seen what is said to be the Kerith Ravine in Israel. The first thing you notice is that it would indeed be a good place to hide. There is almost no way King Ahab could find Elijah in such an area.

Why Is This Important?

God has a plan for your life. His idea for your future is a thousand times better and greater than anything you could come up with on your own. God loves you with an everlasting love (see Jeremiah 31:3); He wants only what is best for you. He will withhold no good thing from you when you seek to do His will above all else (see Psalm 84:11). You may or may not be another Elijah, but God will go to the same pains in preparing you for what He has in mind for you as He did for Elijah.

One's visible profile in the Kingdom of God does not determine the extent of God's love. Not all of us can be Elijahs, but all of us are loved and cared for as much as Elijah. The niche that God has determined for each of us requires preparation so that we will be ready when our ultimate moment comes. Jesus tasted death for every person (see Hebrews 2:9). Moreover, God honors His Son's blood to the hilt, but only when it is embraced by the person who believes. The moment you affirm and embrace the blood of Jesus is when you can be sure that God is on your side.

How do you do this? You must abandon *all* hope in your good works and personal righteousness that you thought would get you to heaven when you die. You then transfer the trust you had in yourself to what Jesus did for you on the cross. You trust His blood—alone. It is then you not only have assurance that you will go to heaven when you die but also know that God is working on your case now.

You and I need to know the next step forward when it comes to God's plan for us. He does not reveal the totality of that plan from A to Z. He leads us from A to B, from B to C, etc. Don't ask, What is Z? Ask, What is B? The next step for Elijah was not to head for Mount Carmel, but to head eastward, cross over the Jordan River and settle in the Kerith Ravine. It would be his next home for a while. Wisdom is having the presence of the mind of the Holy Spirit, which also means knowing the next thing to do.

Elijah's Preservation

Elijah's new home in the Kerith Ravine was not only for his preparation but equally for his protection and preservation. King Ahab would spend the next few years trying to find him. Elijah's word had so infuriated the king—and so threatened him—that Elijah became Public Enemy No. 1, insofar as Ahab was concerned. Had Ahab been right with God, he would have welcomed Elijah's word. Instead of wanting to destroy him, the king should have fallen on his knees and thanked God that there was a prophet in Israel.

Is it not amazing how people want to shoot the messenger when that messenger does not bring good news? Elijah was only relaying the message that was best for Israel. Behind Elijah's prayer that it would not rain was his burden for Israel. He loved his nation. He hated seeing it being taken over by false prophets—evil men who despised God's covenant. Elijah had one goal: to rid Israel of these men. He reckoned that to pray that it might not rain would eventually lead to the confrontation on Mount Carmel, which we will examine later in this book.

God ordered that Elijah be kept in hiding for a long while. There are two kinds of hiding. The first is when someone is running from God. Jonah tried this. God told Jonah to go to Nineveh and Jonah foolishly tried to run from God. The truth is, one cannot really run from God. As the psalmist put it, "If I make my bed in the depths [Hebrew, *sheol*], you are there" (Psalm 139:8). God is everywhere. So while you may *try* to run from God, you will not succeed.

Some people refuse to confess Christ openly lest they bear the reproach of being a true Christian. They choose to remain in hiding. Jesus said that if we are ashamed of Him, He will be ashamed of us (see Mark 8:38). He said that if we will confess Him before men, He will confess us before the Father (see Matthew 10:32). I lovingly urge you, dear reader, to come out of hiding and accept the stigma, the shame and the reproach. Do it now.

The second kind of hiding is when you are hiding from an enemy who is determined to destroy you. This was Elijah's kind. God was on Elijah's side, and gave specific orders to Elijah to head eastward and settle in at the Kerith Ravine. If someone is out to destroy you, listen carefully to the Holy Spirit. He will show you the next step forward. He will protect you, He will preserve you.

If someone is out to get you—not to do bodily harm to you but to hurt your reputation—God has shown the next step forward for you: Do nothing. "Do not take revenge, . . . for it is written: 'It is mine to avenge; I will repay,' says the Lord" (Romans 12:19; see also Deuteronomy 32:35). Let God do the vindicating. Don't deprive God of doing what He does best—to vindicate! If you want to be a fool, try vindicating yourself. God will protect you, preserve you—that is, if you will let Him! God put Elijah in a situation whereby the prophet had no choice but to wait on God.

God sent Elijah to the Kerith Ravine not only to protect him from Ahab but also to preserve him. He needed to develop spiritually and emotionally. He needed to be out of the battle for a while. Confronting a king is no small thing. As soon as Elijah spoke as he did to Ahab, he took off!

We will see this pattern again in Elijah's life. Protection from an evil king is one thing; being preserved so that one can develop spiritually is another. Elijah needed both—these being part of his preparation. This would require patience. "Ye have need of patience," the writer of Hebrews said (Hebrews 10:36, KJV). Don't we all? Elijah would learn to move one step at a time over the next few years.

Elijah's Provisions

There is more. Elijah would need to be provided for. He would need food and water. He was told to go eastward to the Kerith Ravine: "You will drink from the brook, and I have ordered the ravens to feed you there" (1 Kings 17:4). This does not sound like dining at a "Five Star" restaurant, but when there is an impending famine and you are running for your life, having *any* food and water will do nicely! This also shows God's sovereign control over nature: "I have ordered the ravens to feed you there." That seems like pretty good security to me. When God is working on your behalf, relax. Wait. Watch. You have nothing to worry about.

Never, never, never underestimate how God will supply your need. "My God will meet all your needs according to his glorious riches in Christ Jesus" (Philippians 4:19). "Is anything too hard for the LORD?" (Genesis 18:14). He has ways of supplying your need that you never have dreamed of.

I can never forget the autumn of 1963 when Louise and I lived in Carlisle, Ohio. The little church there, of which I was the pastor, rejected my ministry; they stopped their giving and did all they could to get us to leave. It worked, though we struggled for a while before we finally resigned. Ultimately, the treasurer had to say, "There is no money to pay you this week." We woke up the next morning devastated. But in that day's mail we received a check for $25.00—just in the nick of time! The day before in a town three hundred miles away an old friend had said to her husband, "I believe we should send R. T. and Louise a check for $25.00." I did not even think this couple knew where we lived! That check meant the world to us. It taught me that God has a way of supplying our needs that we could not have predicted.

"I have ordered the ravens to feed you there." It is interesting to compare this word to Leviticus 11:13–15: "These are the birds you are to detest and not eat because they are detestable: the eagle, the vulture, the black vulture, the red kite, any kind of black kite, any kind of raven." So think of this: God used ravens to feed Elijah. It is not that Elijah *ate* ravens, but that the ravens were used to bring him food. The ravens would fly into places where there was meat, corn and grain. With God nothing is impossible.

Living in Solitude

Whatever would Elijah do with his time in this ravine east of the Jordan River? All he could do, it would seem, was to drink from the brook and wait for the ravens to bring him food. But what an encouragement to watch this happen morning and evening, morning and evening—ravens coming with more food!

But there is more. Perhaps never again would Elijah have such an opportunity to be utterly *alone*. What do you do when you are alone? By yourself? In solitude? With nothing to do? You pray. And pray. And pray. For all I know, Elijah would never again have these days when there was nothing to do but pray. A person who is highly gifted needs to pray

31

more than anyone. You develop intimacy with your heavenly Father. You develop sensitivity to the Holy Spirit. You get to know God's *ways*. You and I are required to know essentially two things: God's Word and His ways. You know His Word by reading the Bible. You know His ways by spending time with Him.

How much do you pray? When you stand before God at the Judgment Seat of Christ you may have many regrets over how you spent your time, but you will have no regrets over any amount of time you spent in prayer. There will be no praying in heaven. Take advantage of every opportunity to pray—now.

Walking in Obedience

"So he did what the LORD had told him" (1 Kings 17:5). Obedience. That is the secret: Doing what God tells you to do. Nothing more; just *do it*. "He went to the Kerith Ravine, east of the Jordan, and stayed there." He *stayed there*. You do not move until God says to move. You stay there. It is the way the children of Israel were guided in the wilderness: "Whenever the cloud lifted from above the tabernacle, they would set out; but if the cloud did not lift, they did not set out—until the day it lifted" (Exodus 40:36–37).

How do you know what God is saying? First, you get your instructions from Scripture. Elijah did not have the Bible as we have, but he had the Mosaic Law. He was well-versed in the covenant relationship between God and the children of Israel. When a person is immersed in the Word of God, he will have a fairly shrewd idea of how to live. Second, you listen to the impulse of the Holy Spirit. Note the order: the Scriptures first, the impulse second. You are

32

very likely not going to hear God speak to you if you bypass His Word. It is required that you know His Word *so well* that the impulse of the Spirit often merely heightens the knowledge of the Word.

When you are devoted to the Word of God—being fully determined to follow it—God will honor you with the impulse of the Spirit. He begins with Holy Scripture, which He wrote. Never forget that the Holy Spirit wrote the Bible (see 2 Timothy 3:16; 2 Peter 1:21). To get on good terms with the Holy Spirit, you need to extol and embrace the Holy Spirit's greatest product—the Bible. You honor the Holy Spirit when you honor the Bible.

An example of the impulse of the Holy Spirit is when Philip heard God speak to him: "Go south to the road—the desert road—that goes down from Jerusalem to Gaza" (Acts 8:26). Philip obeyed. Soon he noticed a man in a chariot reading from the prophet Isaiah. "The Spirit told Philip, 'Go to that chariot and stay near it'"(verse 29). The eventual consequence of this was the conversion of the man in the chariot.

Philip knew his Bible. The proof: He was able to explain Isaiah 53, which the man in the chariot was reading. In other words, here was a man who knew his Bible backward and forward, and here was a man who obeyed the impulse of the Holy Spirit. God still does this today. God honors men and women with the impulse of His Spirit when they have taken the time to know the Bible.

People ask, Why do I need teaching? Why do I need to read the Bible? I reply: Jesus said that the Holy Spirit would "remind" us of what we have already learned in our hearts (John 14:26). It is not enough to want to be Spirit-filled so you can know the Spirit's impulse. You need to have something in your *mind* that the Holy Spirit can remind you of.

If you are empty-headed before you are Spirit-filled you will be empty-headed afterward! The Holy Spirit brings to your remembrance only the Word that is already there. How did it get there? By diligent, patient and consistent reading of the Bible.

I think a lot of people, especially young Christians, want the impulse of the Spirit but do not know their Bibles. They say they have no time to read the Bible. I tell them: The more you know the Bible, the more you will have the impulse of the Spirit. The less you know the Bible, the less you can expect the impulse of the Spirit. This is because the impulse of the Holy Spirit will always be in accordance with Scripture. God will never give you an impulse that is contrary to what the Holy Spirit has already written in the Bible.

How to Know the Next Step Forward

So how do you know the next step forward? First, you obey immediately what God says initially. *Accept* what He says with delight. "One thing I ask of the LORD, this is what I seek: that I may dwell in the house of the LORD all the days of my life, to gaze upon the beauty of the LORD and to seek him in his temple" (Psalm 27:4).

Second, avoid no detail. God said, "Turn eastward and hide in the Kerith Ravine, east of the Jordan" (1 Kings 17:3). So he went to the Kerith Ravine, east of the Jordan. You do even the least thing He requires. Jesus said that he who is faithful in that which is least is faithful also in much (see Luke 16:10).

Third, allow for no delay. Obey His instructions at once. "So he did what the LORD had told him." There was no waiting.

The God of Elijah is faithful and true; He always keeps His word. Elijah was told to go eastward to the Kerith Ravine to drink of the brook and be fed by the ravens by God's orders. So it followed (surprise, surprise): "The ravens brought him bread and meat in the morning and bread and meat in the evening, and he drank from the brook" (1 Kings 17:6).

3

The Unsurprising Disappointment

> Some time later the brook dried up because there
> had been no rain in the land.
>
> 1 Kings 17:7

Elijah was on a roll. Confidently and boldly he had uttered his word to Ahab, that there would be "neither dew nor rain" unless he ordered it, then he got away without being hurt. He made his way to Kerith Ravine, east of the Jordan. He was protected, preserved and provided for. He had plenty of water and adequate food because the ravens brought him meat and grain. He was no doubt lonely, but he was still feeling pretty good. It is a wonderful feeling when God blesses us this way. In times like this it is easier to trust God for more; indeed, it is far easier to praise and worship God when your needs are being supplied.

So far, so good. But the good feeling was coming to an end. Elijah now had to face a consequence of his own prophecy that he might not have anticipated. He had said it would not rain; it did not. But the eventual result was that, with no rain on the land, there were no trickles of water running down the hills into the brooks. It was only a matter of time before there would be no brooks at all. Indeed, the brook that was Elijah's source of water near the Kerith Ravine dried up. Ravens might have kept coming with food, but one also needs water to survive.

The unsurprising disappointment is this: when one is disappointed, but should have expected it.

Things That Should Not Surprise Us

Certain things should not surprise us. You should not be surprised, for example, when you reap what you sow. "Do not be deceived: God cannot be mocked. A man reaps what he sows" (Galatians 6:7). Furthermore, you should not be surprised at the terrible fallout when a divine warning is ignored, as when God says, "I will laugh at your disaster," to those who reject wisdom and knowledge (see Proverbs 1:20–26). Neither should you be surprised at the consequence of being "stiff-necked after many rebukes" and then being suddenly "destroyed—without remedy" (Proverbs 29:1)—a verse that was invariably preached about in revival campaigns (especially during the final services) in my old church in Ashland, Kentucky. You and I are fools if we think we are exempt from the principles of God's Word being applied to us. God is no respecter of persons.

Still, it is likely that Elijah had not anticipated that his prophecy about rain would mean that he himself would feel the pinch of the famine. He was not exempt. He became a victim of his own prayer and prophecy. He had prayed that it would not rain, and it did not rain. He had prophesied that there would be neither dew nor rain, and there was neither dew nor rain.

But that meant that *he* would not have the benefit of rain, that he, too, would be threatened by famine and would die without water—if he failed to find it somewhere. In Israel there is a rainy season only twice a year. Residents depend on the melting of the snow on Mount Hermon to cause the land to flourish. The melted snow of Mount Hermon is the reason for the Jordan River. No dew, no rain also meant no snow, no brook, no streams, no rivers. If Israel goes a year without rain the Jordan River becomes just a trickle. Imagine it after three years!

This could have been a time of soul-searching for Elijah. "Did I get it wrong by prophesying as I did? Did I make a mistake? What have I done? Am I not the cause of this fam-ine? And now I myself am in trouble." Or did Elijah wonder if God had broken His word? After all, God had promised Elijah that he would drink from the brook, but now there was no brook! God had promised Elijah that he would be taken care of, but that promise was becoming hard to embrace. Or might God make an exception in Elijah's case—to let all *other* brooks and streams dry up, but not the one that ran by the Kerith Ravine? Might God miraculously bring water as He had sent the ravens to feed him? That did not happen. "The brook dried up because there had been no rain in the land."

You can be the greatest prophet on earth, but you need food and water to survive. You can go without food for forty days, but you cannot go much beyond two or three days without water, especially in the climate that exists in Israel. So was God breaking His word? Having promised to take care of him—with food and water—whatever was going on now? "The brook dried up because there had been no rain in the land."

Have you ever experienced a definite leading of the Lord whereby He promised to look after you? All goes well for many a day. Then . . . suddenly things go wrong. Financial reverse. Emotional breakdown. Major health problems. Desertion by friends and supporters. "The brook dried up."

The Betrayal Barrier

"Truly you are a God who hides himself, O God and Savior of Israel" (Isaiah 45:15). Isaiah seems to have discovered this firsthand. The hiding of God's face, when He appears to desert you, makes God seem like an enemy. It is a form of chastening, being disciplined—part of God's preparation. God's chastening is essentially preparation, and that preparation is often carried out by God hiding His face. Indeed, the essence of being disciplined is to experience the hiding of God's face. It isn't fun.

I call it the *betrayal barrier*. It is when God *appears* to betray you. He does not betray you—truly—but He seems to do so. Behind the clouds the sun is always shining, and behind a frowning providence He hides a smiling face.

Question: What do you do when you feel that God has betrayed you?

Answer: Break the betrayal barrier.

In the twentieth century one of the great feats of aeronautical science was when a jet could break the sound barrier—that is, fly faster than the speed of sound. It was a stunning accomplishment. But there is an accomplishment that you and I can pull off—and you do not need to be a scientist. You do not need to have a high IQ. You do not need to be highly educated, cultured or of "good stock" (as they say). Anybody can do it: namely, break the betrayal barrier.

I cannot prove this statistic, but my pastoral experience has taught me that perhaps nine out of ten Christians sooner or later feel that God has let them down. Some actually feel betrayed. He does this at the worst possible time! It is when the brook dries up, and you never had that possibility on your radar screen. It happens to nearly all of us. My pastoral experience also suggests that nine out of ten Christians get angry with God when they feel suddenly deserted by Him. They back off as if to say, "Thanks a lot, God," in a cynical and sarcastic manner.

Sadly, they never know what it would have been like had they lowered their voices, cooled off and waited. For God hides His face from you to give you an opportunity to *break the betrayal barrier*. I reckon that one out of ten breaks the betrayal barrier and discovers what it is like on the other side when you resolve to trust God. If Winston Churchill could address a discouraged Britain in World War II with the words *We shall never, ever surrender! We shall never, ever surrender!* surely the Christian can do this! I go into more detail on this issue in my book *Totally Forgiving God* (Charisma, 2012).

If you are in the midst of a fiery trial—perhaps the greatest trial of your life—resolve right now to break the betrayal barrier. You can do it. Job said, "Though he slay me, yet will I hope in him" (Job 13:15).

Sooner or Later Trouble Comes

My point is this. You and I should not be surprised when trouble comes. "In this world you will have trouble," said

Jesus. "But take heart! I have overcome the world" (John 16:33). Learn not to be surprised—or shaken—by disappointment. Learn not to be surprised when a good person lets you down. I learned a long time ago that when I begin to admire a person a little bit too much, he or she sooner or later disappoints me. It should be an unsurprising disappointment. After all, "Do not put your trust in princes, in mortal men, who cannot save" (Psalm 146:3). Expect the best of people to let you down. Learn not to be surprised by disappointment. For this, too, is by God's appointment. Do not be "unsettled" by trials, for we were "destined for them" (1 Thessalonians 3:3). If you, then, dear reader, are in the greatest trial of your life, *take it with both hands*. Resolve now to dignify this trial. Refuse to complain, murmur or grumble. Hold still and watch: God has a plan.

One of my favorite Arthur Blessitt stories occurred when he was in northern Israel at the start of the rainy season. It was cold. There was no place to put his cross (which he has carried all over the world). Finally he lay on a bench at a bus stop. Then the rain started. He looked at the rain and commanded, "Stop in the name of Jesus!"

What do you suppose happened? Not only did it not stop, but there was a sudden flash of lightning and crashing thunder. The rain poured. Arthur just looked up at the sky and said, "God, I love You." That is a small example of breaking the betrayal barrier.

The Universal Effect

There was a universal effect of Elijah's prophecy. The entire nation of Israel now had to live under God's judgment. That is what the absence of rain was—judgment upon Israel, the prophets of Baal and Ahab. But *all* the people were affected by it, including Elijah. He himself had to live under the effects of God's judgment. Take note of these words from a canonical prophet:

> "If a country sins against me by being unfaithful and I stretch out my hand against it to cut off its food supply and send famine upon it and kill its men and their animals, even if these three men—Noah, Daniel and Job—were in it, they could save only themselves by their righteousness, declares the Sovereign LORD."
>
> Ezekiel 14:13–14

In other words, the presence of a godly man would not be enough to cause God's wrath to pass over a nation. This nation was under judgment and going twenty miles away to a neighboring nation would not help.

Billy Graham told how former United States President Lyndon Johnson wanted him in the White House as often as possible during the Vietnam War. Johnson "liked having a clergyman around," said Billy Graham. But there is no evidence that the presence of a clergyman in the White House made any difference in the war.

The universal effect of Elijah's prophecy is a reminder of the universal effect of sin. The world is filled with different cultures, different races, different levels of education, different accents and different degrees of intelligence. But all have one thing in common: We are sinners. "All have sinned" and come short of the glory of God (Romans 3:23). You may say, "We have the worst people in the world in our town." So what do you do? Move to another town? You will find in a very short period of time that people are the same— sinners. Their hearts are deceitful and desperately wicked (see

Jeremiah 17:9). You cannot travel across a nation or around the world to get away from sin and its effects on society. People are corrupt by nature—in politics, in the churches, in government, in banking and finance, in the media and in the entertainment business.

Does this surprise you? It should not. People may have different cultures, languages and colors, but their hearts toward God, the Bible and true righteousness are the same. We have an expression in the South: "He's a good old boy." But scratch him, rub him the wrong way or criticize him and you will find that he will pounce on you—either verbally or otherwise—before you can count to ten!

When the Brook Dries Up

Do you know what it is like when the brook dries up? When the very source of your livelihood and well-being suddenly disappears? It could be that emotional strength wanes—you are not able to cope as you once did. It may be sudden disappearance of financial support—loss of job or the removal of one whose financial support enabled you to meet your needs. It could be loss of friends who supported you, who were always there when you needed them. We all need friends. What do you do when they are gone? What do you do when your spiritual energy disappears?

"Some time later the brook dried up." When was that? It was a deficiency that came at the wrong time. Have you ever experienced the feeling that "things could not possibly get worse"? *But they did.* You thought you had surely reached "rock bottom," that you had come to the lowest possible point in your life. "This is it," you said. "Things cannot possibly get any worse than this." *But they do.* They come at the

worst time in your life. You said, "I can't take any more."
But you can.

There was no water. Food by tons would have no value.
You need water to survive. If the ravens brought Elijah filet
steaks, fresh vegetables and the best-tasting bread it would
have meant nothing.

Change Comes to Us All Sooner or Later

"Some time later." When? It may have been a month or it
could have been a year. But Elijah was now facing a crisis that
meant a huge change. He probably thought he would stay
in the Kerith Ravine indefinitely. But the brook's drying up
meant a big change in his life. Remember this: Circumstances
will always mean eventual change for all of us. Change means
uprooting from the familiar and comfortable. Paul had to
learn this. Indeed, he said,

> I know what it is to be in need, and I know what it is to have
> plenty. *I have learned* the secret of being content in any and
> every situation, whether well fed or hungry, whether living
> in plenty or in want. I can do everything through him who
> gives me strength.
>
> Philippians 4:12–13, emphasis added

When sudden change catapults you into something new,
remember this: God has a better idea for how you should
spend this time of your life. You may stubbornly say, "I am
going to stay right here where this brook was, no matter
what." But if the brook has dried up, like it or not, you have
to move on. It is God's way of getting your attention.

I referred above to our disappointing experience in Carlisle,
Ohio. When we moved to Carlisle in 1962, I thought it would

be the beginning of the era to which I had looked forward for so long, but it turned out to be a disaster. My closest friend let me down. Our supporters deserted us. The brook dried up.

I can now say that the experience in Ohio, which in one sense was the worst thing that ever happened to us, was the best thing that ever happened to us. We needed not only to move on, but also to be emancipated from a mindset and perspective that would have kept us from ever knowing what God ultimately had in mind for us.

When the brook dries up, we know it is time to move. God has something better in mind. Count on it. He will never leave you nor forsake you (seen Hebrews 13:5). No good thing will He withhold from you when it is God's will you want most of all (see Psalm 84:11). Paul admitted that he had to "learn" the secret of contentment in every situation. So with all of us. That learning process can sometimes be painful, but it is worth all we have to go through to get that knowledge of God's new plan.

The Ultimate Change

But there is another change coming for you and me down the road. Are we ready for this? There will come a day—sooner or later—when God will say, "Your time is up." We all have to die. What is more, *everything* that we are doing in this life should be getting us ready for that day.

So I am now going to ask you: Do you know for sure that if you were to die today, you would go to heaven? It is the most important question anybody can ever ask you. Life at its longest is still short. We may say, "I need more time." The truth is, God gives all of us enough time. We may not be prepared for that last day on earth, but we need to get prepared. All of life is moving toward that "Omega Point" when we stand before God at the Judgment Seat of Christ (see 2 Corinthians 5:10).

So I ask again: Do you know for certain that if you were to die today, you would go to heaven? Now for another question: Suppose you were to stand before God (and you will) and He were to ask you (and He might), "Why should I let you into My heaven?" What would you say? Only one answer will do. I will tell you my answer—and I pray it is yours: *Jesus died on the cross for my sins.* When it comes time to die and you have to make the greatest change of all, be sure that this is your heart-of-hearts answer.

The Honor of God

God's honor was attached to Elijah's testimony. With "no rain in the land" Elijah had to make a decision. The angels were watching. Would he complain? Would he question God? Have you considered your own testimony when the brook dries up and there is no rain? The angels are watching, and, almost certainly, people out there are waiting to see what kind of strength you have when adversity comes.

Elijah's integrity was also at stake. Perhaps he was tempted to go to Ahab and proclaim, "The famine is over. I now pronounce that rain will come." He would not have gotten that impulse from God. Furthermore, as recalcitrant as Elijah might have been, it was no doubt too soon to expect Ahab to be mollified sufficiently to be broken and open to Elijah. The famine would continue. Elijah could not make himself the exception to the rule. He would live under God's judgment along with the rest of the people of Israel. So rather than pray for rain, he waited on God to see what would be—yet again—the next step forward.

When the brook dries up because there is no rain, but you say, "Praise the Lord," you bring great honor to God. Trust Him to show you the next step forward. He will. He is never too early, never too late, but always *just on time*. When God closes a door, He opens a window. Learn to accept the closed door and be prepared for the surprising window that will open. It opened for Elijah and it will open for you.

4

Faith Is Sometimes Spelled *R-I-S-K*

Then the word of the LORD came to him: "Go at once to Zarephath of Sidon and stay there. I have commanded a widow in that place to supply you with food."

So he went to Zarephath. When he came to the town gate, a widow was there gathering sticks. He called to her and asked, "Would you bring me a little water in a jar so I may have a drink?" As she was going to get it, he called, "And bring me, please, a piece of bread."

"As surely as the LORD your God lives," she replied, "I don't have any bread—only a handful of flour in a jar and a little oil in a jug. I am gathering a few sticks to take home and make a meal for myself and my son, that we may eat it—and die."

1 Kings 17:8–12

Having been faced with a dried-up brook—a closed door if there ever was one—Elijah needed a window. He got it: The Lord told him to go to Zarephath of Sidon where a widow would look after him. The ravens and the brook, then, were to be succeeded by a Gentile widow about a hundred miles away.

Zarephath was outside Israel in Gentile territory. It turns out that God had been at work behind the scenes: "I have commanded a widow in that place to supply you with food." When you hear a word like that you might expect that this widow would be waiting as you walk into Zarephath and say, "Welcome, Elijah. God told me you were coming and that I should bless you." Elijah might have been expecting a wealthy widow to welcome him and look after him. A dream situation. No, it did not happen like that.

First, Elijah did not know her name or what she looked like. Second, he had no idea where she lived in this town of Zarephath. He did notice a woman near the town gate gathering sticks—who happened to be a widow. So Elijah asked her for a drink of water, and then a piece of bread. I think this was a rather cheeky thing to do—to ask for water and then to shout out, as she was going to get it, "And bring me, please, a piece of bread." She did not know him; he was "fishing" to see if she was the chosen widow.

She replied, and she did so with what we have defined as *oath* language, very like what Elijah had uttered to Ahab: "As surely as the Lord your God lives, I don't have any bread—only a handful of flour in a jar and a little oil in a jug."

Why did she use language like that? Because she knew that Elijah was from Israel; she referred to "the Lord *your* God." She wanted to convince this man that she was stating the absolute truth! *She was no wealthy widow.* A person usually resorts to speaking an oath only when there may be doubt as to whether or not the truth is being told. She then added: "I am gathering a few sticks to take home and make a meal for myself and my son, that we may eat it—and die" (verse 12).

This was hardly an encouraging response! It was not the kind of welcome Elijah was expecting, but, as a later prophet would say, "Whoever has despised the day of small things shall rejoice" (Zechariah 4:10, esv). Sometimes inauspicious beginnings end up with spectacular endings. This one did.

God's Far-Reaching Love

We will learn in this chapter of 1 Kings 17 the amazing and surprising ways God supplies our needs. But it also demonstrates God's love for *all* peoples, not only Israel. Early in the ministry of our Lord, immediately after He stood in the synagogue and read from Isaiah 61:1–2, which He said meant Himself, Jesus then referred to this very episode in the life of Elijah:

> "I assure you that there were many widows in Israel in Elijah's time, when the sky was shut for three and a half years and there was a severe famine throughout the land. Yet Elijah was not sent to any of them, but to a widow in Zarephath in the region of Sidon."
>
> Luke 4:25–26

Why did Jesus speak those words at that particular time? It was an unsubtle hint that His ministry would be shared with and welcomed by Gentiles. This was too much for the Jews to take. In one moment they regarded His words as "gracious" (Luke 4:22); in the next moment they were "furious" and "drove him out of the town, and took him to the brow of the hill on which the town was built, in order to throw him down the cliff" (Luke 4:28–29). They could not bear the thought of Gentiles being brought into the eternal covenant of God.

Elijah, centuries before, went outside Israel to a Gentile widow under God's special instructions. Who would have known then that this had far-ranging prophetic significance?

The Doctrine of Election

This passage demonstrates further how one who holds the truth must persuade those who do not have it, in order to show what is best for them. It is what every minister has to do—persuade people opposed to the Gospel to realize that they need it. Elijah was gently but boldly having to persuade this widow to do what was contrary to her wishes: share her little bit of food and water with this unknown person. He knew at this early stage in their meeting, though she did not, that it was in her self-interest to do what he said.

There is another reason Elijah put these requests to her. At this point, remember, Elijah was not sure that she was the widow God had in mind. This incident is very like preaching to the lost wherever they are when you know that only God's elect will be saved. Many are called but few are chosen. It is not our job, however, to figure out in advance who the elect are; we present the Word given to us and wait. God's people will respond in due time. Elijah initiated the call. We do the same. We preach the Gospel to everybody, not knowing who will respond. But those whom God has chosen will—sooner or later—say yes to the Holy Spirit. "Those he called, he also justified" (Romans 8:30).

So Elijah became vulnerable, not knowing what the widow's response would be. God's chosen people will often be rebellious at first, putting up arguments against the truth. Saul of Tarsus was like that, but eventually he cried out, "What shall I do, Lord?" (Acts 22:10).

It took courage for Elijah to speak to this widow as he did. He became vulnerable, asking for a drink and some food. He might have gone up to her and said, "Let me introduce myself. I am the prophet Elijah. I am the reason for this famine. I told King Ahab that it would not rain until I said so." No, nothing like that. Moreover, he discovered that this particular woman was needy, negative and noncommittal. She did not say she would help him. She did not realize that this man from Israel was a prophet from the true God, and that he was the best thing that had ever happened to her.

So, in the event that she was the chosen one, he set out to persuade her to trust his word. Elijah said,

> "Don't be afraid. Go home and do as you have said. But first make a small cake of bread for me from what you have and bring it to me, and then make something for yourself and your son. For this is what the LORD, the God of Israel, says: 'The jar of flour will not be used up and the jug of oil will not run dry until the day the LORD gives rain on the land.'"
>
> She went away and did as Elijah had told her. So there was food every day for Elijah and for the woman and her family. For the jar of flour was not used up and the jug of oil did not run dry, in keeping with the word of the LORD spoken by Elijah.
>
> 1 Kings 17:13–16

How to Experience Extraordinary Things

At this point we see something extraordinary. Elijah began to discern that this woman was the widow God had appointed.

So, with boldness, he then asked her to make a cake of bread for himself *before* making one for her and her son. Elijah's cheekiness was now doubled! How could he do that to a poor, needy Gentile widow, who had no ample supply of food for herself and her child? He could do that because he knew God would do the rest—persuade the widow (if she was indeed the chosen one) to do what Elijah had requested. There is an old song that says, "God doesn't compel us against our will, but makes us willing to go." This is called *effectual calling*.

So now Elijah—all of a sudden—instead of being cared for by her had to build her up. "Don't be afraid. The jar of flour will not be used up and the jug of oil will not run dry until the day the Lord gives rain on the land." We do not know why this Gentile widow should have believed this, but she did. "She went away and did as Elijah had told her."

This part of the Elijah story is important because it not only continues to demonstrate patience in disappointment but also shows how faith is sometimes spelled *R-I-S-K*. *Risk* means "to accept or expose yourself to possible harm or loss." So the question becomes, Who took the greater risk, Elijah or the widow? Elijah risked being extremely impertinent and putting her off entirely. The widow risked depleting her last bit of food.

Going Outside Your Comfort Zone

Behind this part of the story is a principle of faith: To experience the extraordinary you must go outside your comfort zone. Do you want to see God work in a powerful way—as in the days of the earliest Church? I ask you: Do you want things to go on as usual, or do you want to see God do something unusual? If you want to see the extraordinary, I have to tell you that it means going outside your comfort zone. I wish it were not that way, but it is! Every person God used in the Old Testament and the New Testament and in Church history over the last two thousand years has had to go outside his or her comfort zone. That is partly why faith is sometimes spelled R-I-S-K.

I would say this to you: If you get a clear invitation to move outside your comfort zone because of the possibility you might see God do the unusual, take it with both hands!

And yet this part of the story shows that God supplies our need in a way that is both extraordinary but also ordinary. The extraordinary: The flour and oil were never used up. The ordinary: There was just enough for each day. It was never a case of a hundred barrels of flour and oil being wasted before their eyes. The amount was small and always there. Enough is enough. You do not need flour and oil for tomorrow; only for today. You can live only one day at a time. You can take only one bite at a time. What more could you cope with anyway? My dad's favorite verse was, "Seek first his kingdom and his righteousness, and all these things will be given to you as well" (Matthew 6:33). The next verse goes on to say, "Therefore do not worry about tomorrow, for tomorrow will worry about itself."

Dr. A. W. Pink observed that this command—to make the cake for Elijah first and then for her and her son—was one of the hardest commandments ever given. And, yet, for her to grant it was equally hard. It meant *both* of them going outside their comfort zones. Elijah wanted to confirm beyond all doubt that she was truly the widow God had chosen to supply his needs. He was gentle with her: "Don't be afraid," he said.

In the process, then, Elijah put obstacles in her way in order to be sure. He might have said, "Make a cake for yourself and your son, and then make some for me." That would have been considered more sensible and unselfish. But, no, she was required to make this for him *first*—and then she and her son could have some.

Added to his request was Elijah's odd claim that this came from the "God of Israel" (1 Kings 17:14). This made the challenge even harder for this Gentile widow. Have you any idea how much the ancient Gentiles in that part of the world hated Israel? They did then and they do now. Elijah, thus, added to the obstacle he had put in her way.

Granted, the widow had nothing to lose. It was the best offer she had. So, too, with receiving the Gospel message. You are going to die anyway. This is decreed for us all, for it is appointed unto all men and women "to die once, and after that to face judgment" (Hebrews 9:27). It is the best offer you are going to get in this world.

It may seem unreasonable—that the blood of Jesus could wash away your sins—but it is the only hope you have. Accept this offer now. Confess your sins to God. Thank Him for sending His Son. Transfer the trust you have in your good works to what Jesus did for you on the cross. Doing this will result in a pardon of all your sins. When the widow did what Elijah said to do, all he promised came to pass. It will with you, too, when you affirm this Gospel.

5

Coping with Being Misunderstood

> Some time later the son of the woman who owned the house became ill. He grew worse and worse, and finally stopped breathing. She said to Elijah, "What do you have against me, man of God? Did you come to remind me of my sin and kill my son?" "Give me your son," Elijah replied.
>
> 1 Kings 17:17–19

Some time later indicates that the woman and her son did not die from starvation (as she had feared) for Elijah's promise had proved true: Flour and oil were supplied day after day after day. But some time later—perhaps after weeks, months or years—the widow's son died. She blamed Elijah for this. And yet it was Elijah's coming to Zarephath that kept them alive during this period. Instead of being grateful for what he had done for her she now accused him. Their relationship was moving into a new phase.

Three Phases of Relationships

Gerald Coates says all new relationships go through three phases: (1) *veneer* (which often seems lyrical), when you think you have met the greatest person or friend in the entire world; (2) *disillusionment*, when you feel totally let down if not betrayed by this person; and (3) *reality*, when you have an objective perception about this person.

The widow of Zarephath was now in phase two of her relationship with Elijah. She had likely thought not only that his very presence guaranteed the survival of her and her son, but also that nothing negative could happen to her as long as Elijah was around. This was an unfair assumption; such feelings were almost superstitious. Still, it was the way she felt. She had a false dependence upon him.

The widow said to Elijah, "What do you have against me, man of God? Did you come to remind me of my sin and kill my son?" This is disillusionment language—emotional, full of self-pity and panic.

This was not an easy moment for Elijah. This part of the story shows something of the suffering of a true prophet. It is true that the greater the suffering the greater the anointing, but it is also true that the greater the anointing, the greater the suffering. Never forget this. Anointing carries suffering with it. It was true of Abraham. It was true of Moses. Not only did Elijah experience his own sense of being let down by God when the brook dried up, but now he has an unanticipated crisis on his hands: a distraught widow who has suddenly lost her only son—and Elijah to blame.

Disillusioned with a True Man of God?

Have you ever experienced this? That you felt as though you had just met the greatest human being who ever lived, only to be completely let down (and to begin to suspect evil things)? This does not apply just to people. You might have felt this way about a new job, a new place to live, a new church or a new phase of your life.

It is quite possible to be sincerely disillusioned with a true man or woman of God. This is almost always not the fault of the ones we admire, because we impute perfection to people like this. When you see individuals at a distance, admiring and appreciating them, you sometimes imagine more than can possibly be true of *any* human being.

This is a mistake I have made. I grew up admiring preachers. My dad used to introduce me to famous pastors when I was a child. It made me admire them—those with national profile and those who were my pastors in my old church in Kentucky. But then when I saw a fault in them it sometimes devastated me. It was not their fault, but nonetheless that is the way I felt. We should accept this as a truism sooner than later: The best of people are going to let you down. As it has been said many times, "The best of men are men at best."

There is one person who will never let you down, will never fail you. Jesus Christ. He is perfect. Sinless. Faultless. He loves you more than you love yourself. He is always there. Always watching you. Never turning an eye from you. He loves you as though there were no other person to love. He will never, never, never fail you. Ever. Count on it. My whole life and ministry are based upon this premise: the absolute, unwavering perfection of Jesus.

Patience with the Suffering

An unexpected grief came to this widow of Zarephath, and, through it, an unexpected trial came to Elijah. God did not tell Elijah this would happen. But remember: Elijah himself was still in preparation. We must never assume that someone's amazing gift means that he or she is ready for everything that is coming down the road. The brilliant gift may be unimprovable, but the person who has the gift may need a lot of further instruction, discipline, chastening and growing through perplexing situations.

The hiding of God's face is the essence of His discipline. Moreover, God never gives advanced warning when He will be hiding His face. If only He would say, "Next Tuesday about 3:20 P.M., you will notice that the light of My countenance will be withdrawn for a while." If only. Then we could be ready and not be shaken. But part of our preparation is learning how to respond in impossible situations when God seems very far away.

And yet the widow was understandably in grief. We do and say strange things—sometimes bizarre things—when we are swallowed up in grief. No one should be hard on us when we say thoughtless and selfish things when we are in grief. Both Mary and Martha accused Jesus of being the cause of their brother's death by not responding immediately to their request: "Lord, if you had been here, my brother would not have died" (John 11:21, 32). Jesus did not rebuke either of them. Instead, He wept with them (see John 11:35). So with all of us. He knows our frame; He remembers we are dust.

This is a reminder that not all is rosy merely because we are Christians. Do not come to Christ expecting that you will never have a problem again! One of my most memorable converts—the first person I baptized at Westminster

59

Chapel—said to me, "Things got worse, not better, for me after I became a Christian." But he never gave up.

The widow of Zarephath was bitter in her grief. She became sarcastic: "What do you have against me, man of God?" Bitterness always seems justified at first. When we lose our tempers we often think we are quite right to feel what we feel and say what we say. This widow would eventually be sorry. We all are. And yet she went still further—accusing Elijah of *killing* her son: "Did you come to remind me of my sin and kill my son?" In this moment she forgot all that Elijah had done since he arrived in Zarephath.

The widow's comments are typically what most people feel at difficult times. First, she wondered if it was some sin in her life that brought this. We all have things in our pasts that we are ashamed of. We all have skeletons in the closet. And we often fear that God is somehow "getting even" with us by bringing some calamity or disaster our way. Second she accused Elijah of killing her son, which is the way many treat God. They want to accuse God of doing things that bring us grief in order to make Him look bad. This was a horrible thing for her to do, to lay this guilt on Elijah himself.

Elijah Responded Well

Elijah was brilliant in his response. He did not panic. He did not moralize with the distraught widow. He did not say, "I can't believe you are talking to me like this." He did not retort, "How dare you speak like this, seeing how the flour and the oil keep you alive!" He did not give her a guilt trip as she was trying to do to him. He merely said, "Give me your son."

When we can achieve calm and repose while those around us are losing their heads and blaming things on us, we are beginning to grow.

But there is another dimension to this scenario—namely, Elijah having to cope when he was misunderstood. Gerald Coates reckons that the curse of our generation is the desire to be understood. The truth is, the greatest people have had to cope with being misunderstood.

What do you do when you are misunderstood? Elijah impressively set a standard for how one should respond when this happens. He did not defend himself. He did not panic. He did not say, "Oh, dear, I must not be a man of God after all!" No. "Give me your son," he said to the widow. The greatest freedom is having nothing to prove. He did not take her tantrum personally. He did not focus on the woman, but on the child.

> He took him from her arms, carried him to the upper room where he was staying, and laid him on his bed. Then he cried out to the LORD, "O LORD my God, have you brought tragedy also upon this widow I am staying with, by causing her son to die?" Then he stretched himself out on the boy three times and cried to the LORD, "O LORD my God, let this boy's life return to him!"
>
> The LORD heard Elijah's cry, and the boy's life returned to him, and he lived. Elijah picked up the child and carried him down from the room into the house. He gave him to his mother and said, "Look, your son is alive!"
>
> Then the woman said to Elijah, "Now I know that you are a man of God and that the word of the LORD from your mouth is the truth."
>
> 1 Kings 17:19–24

Elijah was vindicated openly in the widow's eyes. The pity is, she should have known this already by now. The bread and oil being kept constant should have been enough. It took a further and greater miracle—which also defied natural explanation—to convince her. So with many in the Last Day regarding Jesus. When "every eye will see him" (Revelation 1:7), Jesus will be openly vindicated, for *all* on that day will say, "Now I know." But that knowledge will not be graced with the title *faith*. It will be too late for faith; it will be sight.

The vindication for Elijah was wonderful. But he did not get his question answered: "O Lord, my God, have you brought tragedy upon this widow I am staying with, by causing her son to die?" Perhaps he was as perplexed as this widow! He was saying virtually the same thing to the Lord as she had said to him. The great prophet did not know the answer either! The best of God's servants have their questions. The greatest theologians have their questions.

Answers to Questions and Prayers

Elijah's question was not answered, but his prayer was. Which would you prefer, an answer to your question or an answer to your prayer? I am sure that the widow did not particularly want her question answered; she wanted her son back, and that is what she got. Had Elijah waited for his question to be answered he would have never prayed. I have had countless people say to me, "When God explains to me why He allows suffering I will believe in Him." The result in that case will be that you will *never* know the answer to that question here on earth. So are you going to lose your soul and be eternally lost? Or will you pray the prayer, "God be merciful to me a sinner," without your questions being answered?

Elijah also wanted the problem solved more than he wanted the answer to his question. Are you, too, willing, then, for

God to answer your prayer without your getting all your questions answered? Elijah wanted the crisis to be dealt with, and the boy was raised from the dead. Answered prayer is better—and more important—than answered questions.

Answers *will* eventually come to the person who chooses answered prayer over answered questions. And they will also get their questions answered—eventually. You will get your answer in heaven. In the words of an old southern Gospel song, in heaven "I'll ask the reasons—He'll tell me why."

As for Elijah's manner of praying, it was odd to say the least. He stretched himself out on the boy's body three times. Why? You tell me! All I know is, that is what he did. Then he cried out—perhaps he cried out three times as well—"Let this boy's life return to him!" Jesus said we should always pray and not give up (see Luke 18:1). There is nothing wrong with praying the same request over and over again. Elijah's prayer was answered—but not his question.

Elijah was vindicated then and there as being a true man of God. Not everybody gets vindication that soon. For some it takes years. For some, vindication takes place after he or she has gone to heaven. Jesus never was universally vindicated—on earth, that is. His vindication was "by the Spirit" (1 Timothy 3:16). One day He will be openly vindicated—when every knee shall bow and every tongue confess that He is Lord (see Philippians 2:11). Every person will then say, "Now I know." But until that final day, Jesus will remain the most misunderstood and "unvindicated" person who ever lived.

6

When Things Start Happening Again

> After a long time, in the third year, the word of the
> LORD came to Elijah: "Go and present yourself to
> Ahab, and I will send rain on the land." So Elijah
> went to present himself to Ahab.
>
> 1 Kings 18:1–2

You may recall that we raised the question, Whose idea was it that it would not rain: God's or Elijah's? The answer? The buck stops with *God*. Further evidence of this is the verse we study in this chapter. Elijah did not go to Ahab to say it would rain; he waited to hear from God. He waited a long time—three and a half years. Then one day the word of the Lord came to Elijah to present himself to Ahab. And from that moment things started happening.

You and I cannot make things happen. Elijah could not make things happen. We are fools if we try to make things happen in our own strength. I once asked the late Carl F. H. Henry, called "the dean of American theologians," what he would do differently if he had his life to live over. After a moment he replied, "I would remember that only God can turn the water into wine." The greatest folly you and I can give in to is running ahead of God to make it look as though we are telling God what to do next.

Waiting on God is one of the hardest things in this world to do. That means virtually *doing nothing* until He gives the signal. Part of the genius of Elijah is that he did nothing until God gave the word. As the psalmist put it, "My soul waits for the Lord more than watchmen wait for the morning" (Psalm 130:6). "As the eyes of slaves look to the hand of their master [watching for him to send the signal], . . . so our eyes look to the LORD our God, till he shows us his mercy" (Psalm 123:2). This manifestation of mercy is worth waiting for.

Seasons Are God's Idea

The God of the Bible often chooses to do things in "seasons." On the fourth day of creation, God said, "Let there be lights in the expanse of the sky to separate the day from the night, and let them serve as signs to mark *seasons* and days and years" (Genesis 1:14, emphasis added). The seasons—spring, summer, autumn and winter—are God's idea. "He has shown kindness by giving you rain from heaven and crops in their seasons" (Acts 14:17).

So, too, at the spiritual level. God has chosen to show up in "seasons." He does not tell us the dates of such manifestation in advance, but He does promise "times of refreshing" (Acts 3:19). We are admonished to "be prepared in season and out of season" (2 Timothy 4:2).

Being "in season" is when God makes Himself *real*. It is when praying comes easily, when talking to people about Christ seems effortless, when conversions happen suddenly. Those are wonderful times.

Being "out of season" is when God hides Himself, when praying and reading your Bible are hard. It is *between the times*, to use Richard Bewes' phrase, when nothing seems to be happening. And yet Paul says be ready, prepared "in season and out of season." It is not unlike being prepared for the Second Coming; we do not know the day nor the hour (see Matthew 24:44). So also when God suddenly shows up in our lives. He wants us to stay ready. Just as the Second Coming is set in advance, by God's design, so, too, the times when God shows up. We cannot make them happen.

Important things happen "between the times." We learn to listen to God. We show how much God means to us by persisting in faith. We get to know God by spending time with Him, even if we cry out, "How long, O LORD?" (Psalm 13:1).

I can never forget what it was like when I was a door-to-door vacuum cleaner salesman. While I longed to be in full-time ministry—knowing all my old friends were in such ministry—I was knocking on doors of strangers to sell them a cleaner they were not in the market for. I thought the era would never end! But I look back on those precious days when I learned so much about so many things that were not academic but practical. It was vital to my preparation.

A Wonderful Opportunity

A huge difference between "in season" and "out of season" is this: "In season" is when God pleases you; "out of season" is when you have a golden opportunity to please God. You may think you are pleasing God when He shows up "in season," but, closer to the truth, He is pleasing you.

When He hides His face, you should seize such a time with both hands. You may never have an opportunity like that again. It is then you please God *by faith*. Persistent faith—the faith that is exhibited by those stalwarts described in Hebrews 11—is what you are called to exercise. Without faith it is impossible to please Him. The one who comes to God "must believe that he exists"—that He "is"—and that He "rewards those who earnestly seek him" (Hebrews 11:6). The reward is worth waiting for.

I do not think Elijah was happy when the brook dried up or when he lived in a Gentile town with a poor widow and her son. But Elijah stayed ready. So after a "long time" God gave him a tap on the shoulder: "Rain is coming at last. Present yourself to Ahab." Things were starting to happen again!

Walking into the Unknown

Now, notice the order in which things began to happen: Elijah had to meet Ahab *before* God sent rain. Elijah might have said to God, "Oh, please let it rain first. Don't make me face Ahab before it starts raining!" The last person Elijah wanted to see was Ahab. Elijah was the most hunted man in Israel. He had no doubt envisaged that God would send rain and then he could turn up immediately and say, "See there? I just prayed that it would rain." No, Elijah was told to present himself to Ahab when the famine was at its worst, and Ahab's anger was at its height.

To put it another way: Elijah had to walk into a dangerous situation. This may seem unfair. Surely he had suffered enough. Surely he had waited long enough. Surely he had proved himself. Elijah's preparation was still going on, and he had to submit as an obedient son to the Father's command.

Apart from Elijah's further preparation, there was a divine strategy behind all that was happening. There always is. God is always at work. Jesus said this of His Father—that He is "always" at work (John 5:17). It is easy to see that He is at work during those glorious "in season" times, but God is also at work when He is hiding His face during those "out of season" times. There is never a day—or a split second in a day—when God is not working. So remember that if He seems to be hiding His face as you read these lines, He not only has a purpose in it but is at work in your life!

> Now the famine was severe in Samaria, and Ahab had summoned Obadiah, who was in charge of his palace. (Obadiah was a devout believer in the LORD. While Jezebel was killing off the LORD's prophets, Obadiah had taken a hundred prophets and hidden them in two caves, fifty in each, and had supplied them with food and water.) Ahab had said to Obadiah, "Go through the land to all the springs and valleys. Maybe we can find some grass to keep the horses and mules alive so we will not have to kill any of our animals." So they divided the land they were to cover, Ahab going in one direction and Obadiah in another.
>
> 1 Kings 18:2–6

The Godly in Strategic Places

In what might be regarded as a parenthetical section of the Elijah story, we learn that Elijah was not the only man of God around. It turns out that Obadiah, a devout follower of the Lord, was in charge of the palace, and had Ahab's trust. (This is not the same Obadiah as the canonical prophet.)

Sometimes God puts holy people in strategic places. Such people are often unsung heroes and are among the bravest people in the world. This section also anticipates Elijah's imperfections. Whereas he will later claim that he alone is left, this section shows how wrong Elijah was—and how inexcusable that he should make that claim.

This section also shows the extent of the famine, as well as how godless the palace was. When one remembers that the great King David, a man after God's own heart, once sat on this very throne, it makes us see how wicked people can eventually succeed the godly.

Jezebel had been killing off the Lord's prophets, but God raised up Obadiah right under her nose. How courageous was this man, who hid a hundred true prophets in caves and provided them with food and water! This part of the story shows how God has placed and preserves His elect all over the globe, often in surprising places. He never leaves Himself without a witness. Just when we might think there are no more devout believers around, we often discover that God has raised up surprising people in unexpected places.

We learn, too, in this section how godly people in unholy places need a lot of wisdom. There is a time to shout out our witness for Jesus, but also a time to protect our testimony by a discreet silence. In other words, there are exceptions to the biblical principle of acknowledging Jesus Christ and showing openly that we are unashamed of Him (see Matthew 10:32–33). Obadiah shows us one such exception. He needed to restrain himself and literally keep quiet for the glory of God. Nicodemus was also a secret believer for a while, though he eventually came out of hiding (see John 3:2; 19:39). We must not judge any, particularly in the Arab world, who are believers in Jesus Christ the Son of God, but may choose to remain silent for a while.

We learn from this also that we should pray for the Obadiahs of this world—those in high places who have had influence for the Lord but who remain discreet and quiet lest this influence be lost. Paul refers to people in his day that may have been in this position (see Philippians 4:22). There is reason to believe that Theophilus, to whom the books of Luke and Acts were written (see Luke 1:3; Acts 1:1), was in this category.

Obadiah was a faithful man; he did everything Ahab told him to do. "Go through the land to all the springs," the king ordered, "to see if grass can be found to keep the mules and horses alive." He was a fervent man—a "devout believer in the Lord." He was also a fearless man. He hid a hundred of the Lord's prophets in caves.

Obadiah was an important person behind the scenes. Low profile, yes, but needed. Such people are always needed when God begins to move after things have not been happening. Though this was a stressful time for Obadiah and Elijah, things were starting to happen again.

7

When God Seems Unfair

As Obadiah was walking along, Elijah met him. Obadiah recognized him, bowed down to the ground, and said, "Is it really you, my lord Elijah?"

"Yes," he replied. "Go tell your master, 'Elijah is here.'"

"What have I done wrong," asked Obadiah, "that you are handing your servant over to Ahab to be put to death? As surely as the LORD your God lives, there is not a nation or kingdom where my master has not sent someone to look for you. And whenever a nation or kingdom claimed you were not there, he made them swear they could not find you. But now you tell me to go to my master and say, 'Elijah is here.' I don't know where the Spirit of the LORD may carry you when I leave you. If I go and tell Ahab and he doesn't find you, he will kill me. Yet I your servant have worshiped the LORD since my youth. Haven't you heard, my lord, what

> I did while Jezebel was killing the prophets of the
> LORD? I hid a hundred of the LORD's prophets in
> two caves, fifty in each, and supplied them with
> food and water. And now you tell me to go to my
> master and say, 'Elijah is here.' He will kill me!"
> Elijah said, "As the LORD Almighty lives, whom
> I serve, I will surely present myself to Ahab today."
>
> 1 Kings 18:7–15

There are no accidents with God. During the time Obadiah and Ahab were looking for grass to feed the mules and horses, lo and behold, Obadiah accidentally ran into Elijah.

At first Obadiah could not believe (what might appear to be) his bad luck! "Is that really you, my lord Elijah?" When Obadiah saw the great Elijah, he panicked. Ahab was looking high and low all over Israel and the surrounding nations for Elijah; Obadiah would be in most serious trouble to be seen with Elijah for it might look as if Obadiah were in league with the prophet and defying the king. You will recall that Obadiah, a devout believer, was strategically placed in Ahab's palace. Obadiah had to be loyal to Ahab—although his ultimate loyalty was to God.

No worries. Elijah assured Obadiah—with an oath—that he would go to Ahab immediately.

The Use of the Oath Again

You will recall that in ancient times the oath, which names a greater authority, was full assurance that one was telling the absolute truth. The exercise of the oath is mentioned twice in this section. First, whenever a nation or kingdom claimed Elijah was not hiding there, Ahab made them *swear* to this. We do not know what greater authority he made them swear by. Second, Elijah swore an oath to Obadiah, "As the Almighty lives, whom I serve, I will surely present myself to Ahab today." Elijah, thus, swore by the name of God.

As soon as Elijah revealed himself to Obadiah, he gave Obadiah a difficult task: "Go tell your master, 'Elijah is here.'" This was a very hard word indeed. Obadiah explained to Elijah that going to Ahab with this information would be signing his own death warrant. "If I go and tell Ahab and he doesn't find you, he will kill me." Obadiah was understandably afraid that Elijah might mysteriously disappear, leaving him in a very vulnerable situation.

This conversation shows that Ahab was obsessed with Elijah. Ahab ought to have been concerned about the God of Israel who brought on the famine. Instead, he was insanely angry with Elijah. It also reminds us of how obsessed King Saul was with David (see 1 Samuel 18:8–16), fearing the young anointed slayer of Goliath more than the Philistines—Israel's chief enemy!

It demonstrates further how those in ultimate authority— whether kings or dictators—often live paranoid lives. They can be utterly preoccupied with the loyalty of those under them, and assume they can sense the slightest sign of disloyalty a mile away. These types of leaders, therefore, live in fear day and night. This ensures that their staff, servants or employees also live in fear day and night, lest they make the slightest unguarded comment that might indicate anything other than sheer adulation.

This kind of situation somehow makes me think of Upton Sinclair's shrewd observation that "it is difficult to get a man to understand something if his salary depends upon his not understanding." People obviously want to keep their jobs, and their security is often attached to their show of loyalty.

Obadiah was at pains to show Elijah that they were on the same side of the issue. "I, your servant, have worshiped the Lord since my youth," Obadiah said. "Haven't you heard, my lord, what I did while Jezebel was killing the prophets of the Lord?"—namely, hide a hundred of the Lord's prophets in two caves and provide for them.

It was at this juncture that Elijah promised to turn himself in to King Ahab, swearing an oath to Obadiah: "As the Lord Almighty lives, whom I serve, I will surely present myself to Ahab today."

Anxiety and the Providence of God

What appeared to be sheer coincidence, then, that Elijah and Obadiah should meet, was in God's providence. The providence of God refers to His sovereign guidance, and, particularly, the ways in which He opens and closes doors. When God closes a door, you are foolish if you try to knock it down; when He opens a door you are likewise foolish if you do not seize the moment and walk through it. As I said, there are no accidents with God. He moves in a mysterious way His wonders to perform, as William Cowper put it. Never underestimate the unseen hand of God.

The best of God's people have fears, of course. Obadiah was a devout follower of the Lord God, but was terrified at the thought of being seen with Elijah at that moment. Never put yourself down merely because you have fears and anxieties. We all have them. Even the great apostle Paul—who told us not to be anxious about anything—was himself so overcome with anxiety when looking for Titus that he consciously turned down a chance to preach in the meantime (see 2 Corinthians 2:12–13).

Being nervous or scared does not mean you are not a Christian or that you do not love the Lord. Some people are prone to timidity from their parents or by early childhood traumas. Do not listen to the devil, the accuser (see Revelation 12:10), when he makes you feel second class because of your fears. Obadiah greatly loved the Lord, but he was terrified when he saw Elijah. The Lord knows our frame and remembers we are dust. Not only that, He invites us to cast all our care and anxiety upon Him because He cares for us (see 1 Peter 5:7). When Jesus sees you in a state of fear He does not moralize and say, "Shame, shame, shame." No. He is touched with the "feeling" of our weaknesses (see Hebrews 4:15, KJV).

As soon as Obadiah saw Elijah, he feared that he was being handed over to Ahab to die, and he turned inward: "What have I done wrong?" Then Obadiah showed further weakness, imagining there was some sin in his life that he should face such a trial. So often we tend to blame ourselves for any negative thing that comes our way—"What have I done wrong?"—as if God is getting ready to punish us. Even Obadiah, devout though he was, had that thought. So if you have this tendency, know you are in good company!

The truth is, Elijah was probably more scared than Obadiah! He wanted Obadiah to pave the way, perhaps forestalling Ahab's wrath. It all goes to show that—as we have said—the best of men are men at best. Nobody is perfect.

Degrees of Anointing

I am sure that Obadiah loved the Lord as much as Elijah did. One's profile in the Kingdom of God or in the Church does not necessarily indicate how personally devoted one is to Christ. Obadiah had a fair measure of profile, yes, being in the palace, but who remembers Obadiah when you consider the story and stature of Elijah? It is quite possible to be intensely devout and unwaveringly faithful and have a low profile. If such a person happens to have a big ego, it can be painful and challenging to stay truly humble and accept little or no visible profile.

And it would not greatly surprise me to learn (especially when we get to heaven) that those with the high profile in the Church and the world were not always the most faithful, godly and devoted servants of Christ. God is sovereign: "No one from the east or the west or from the desert can exalt a man. But it is God who judges; he brings one down, he exalts another" (Psalm 75:6–7). Not only that, the gifts and calling of God are irrevocable (see Romans 11:29) and do not necessarily indicate a close walk with the Lord. There are parts of the body you do not see, says Paul—the kidneys, pancreas and intestines, for instance—but they are as vital to the body as the head, the hand or the eye (see 1 Corinthians 12:21–26).

When God Seems Unfair

It is one of God's ways that He puts difficult requests to us. God told Abraham to sacrifice Isaac, his one and only son and the sole link to the promise of a seed as numerable as the stars in the heavens (see Genesis 22:1–12). God ordered Samuel to go to the house of Jesse to anoint the next king—when King Saul was very much alive. "Saul will hear about it and kill me," said Samuel (1 Samuel 16:2). The angel told Joseph to accept Mary as his wife although she was pregnant—and Joseph knew he was not the father (see Matthew 1:20). Obadiah had to report volatile news to his angry master. Elijah had to come out of hiding—with a price on his head.

The truth is, in the end, God is not unreasonable with any of us. He is testing us along the way to see if we will be true to Him. The most unfair event in the history of the world was when Jesus was sentenced to die on a cross without a fair trial. It was heinous what His enemies did to Jesus. No injustice on earth can be compared to it. But after Jesus was raised from the dead it became clear that God was at the bottom of it all (see Acts 2:23); it was His plan to save the world.

When God seems unfair, remember: He is not unfair. He is faithful and just, sinless and perfect. The day will come when God will clear His name. If we will lower our voices and not judge before God finally steps in, we will be thrilled beyond measure—and have peace along the way.

8

God's Troubler

> So Obadiah went to meet Ahab and told him, and Ahab went to meet Elijah. When he saw Elijah, he said to him, "Is that you, you troubler of Israel?"
>
> "I have not made trouble for Israel," Elijah replied. "But you and your father's family have. You have abandoned the LORD's commands and have followed the Baals. Now summon the people from all over Israel to meet me on Mount Carmel. And bring the four hundred and fifty prophets of Baal and the four hundred prophets of Asherah, who eat at Jezebel's table."
>
> So Ahab sent word throughout all Israel and assembled the prophets on Mount Carmel.
>
> 1 Kings 18:16–20

Elijah got his way: Obadiah went first to approach King Ahab. It would appear that Elijah did not actually go to the palace, but that Ahab "went to meet Elijah" at some designated place. Obadiah, in any case, paved the way.

Ahab's first comment to the illustrious prophet was, "Is that you, you troubler of Israel?" Ahab apparently feared that more bad news was at hand, and he wanted to blame Elijah for all the difficulty Israel was facing. He was giving Elijah a nickname that—in Ahab's reckoning—fit. Ahab was actually nervous to face Elijah.

This was the most wonderful compliment that could have been paid to Elijah. I cannot think of anything more honoring to God than to be addressed like that. I would be thrilled to my fingertips if I were such a threat to the forces of evil that I would be called a "troubler" in a secular, godless world.

It reminds me of the demon who answered the seven sons of Sceva who were trying to cast out the demonic "in the name of Jesus, whom Paul preaches." The evil spirit replied, "Jesus I know, and I know about Paul, but who are you?" (Acts 19:13–15). The forces of evil were unaware of the sons of Sceva—who were obviously no threat to them; but they certainly knew about Jesus and Paul. They were a real threat to the demonic world. As my old friend Rolfe Barnard used to say, "I want to be known in hell." Elijah was known in hell. He was God's "troubler." Are you?

Elijah had been in hiding for three years. He was the most hunted man in that part of the world. But the time had come: God had begun to work, and Elijah turned himself in, as it were. "Is that you?" is the same expression Obadiah had used when he saw Elijah.

Elijah responded this way to Ahab: "I have not made trouble for Israel." It is often true that the very people who are the real cause of the problem blame others. And yet it is likely that Ahab was such a prisoner of his own unbelief that he was unable to see objectively what was actually going on all over Israel: the judgment of God. This, too, is often the case—that calling for a nation to repent because of God's judgment on it usually gets nowhere when the people of that nation have no fear of God. This is where many nations are today, in my opinion.

I also suspect that one of the reasons for the superficiality of today's Church is that there are so few of God's troublers around. My predecessor, Dr. Martyn Lloyd-Jones, used to say that the problem with the modern ministry is that it has too many "nice men." These men are not bad people; they are affable, courteous, gentle, dignified and pleasant. They never put a foot wrong. They never offend. Nice men.

What Nicknames Signify

So Elijah had a new nickname: *troubler of Israel*. We never get the nickname we like! The early believers in Jesus Christ were called "Christians"—a derisive term, not meaning to flatter (see Acts 11:26). They, too, were called troublers; they were described as those who had "caused trouble" all over the world (Acts 17:6). And yet Peter instructed the early Jewish believers not to be ashamed of the name *Christian* (see 1 Peter 4:16).

One should not be ashamed of a stigma, whatever it may be, when it is owing to following Jesus Christ. Those who maintained that the Church of England had not gone far enough in the Great Reformation were dubbed "Puritans." Those in the Holy Club at Oxford, whose members included John Wesley, Charles Wesley and George Whitefield, were mockingly called "Methodists" because of their methods in having set times for prayer. God's chief instruments will be called troublers for God.

God frequently uses most those who are hated most! They can be trusted since they do not cater to people pleasing. If the world hates you because of your faith and love for truth, welcome it; this could mean you have been chosen for a special task. When Peter and John left the Sanhedrin—after being beaten and scolded—they had to pinch themselves because it seemed too good to be true. They literally rejoiced that they were counted worthy to suffer disgrace for "the Name" (Acts 5:41). Be glad if you are upgraded to the status of being God's troubler.

Remember, too, that your ministry will make people feel uneasy. The primary work of the Holy Spirit is to convict of sin (see John 16:8). Thus, His initial work often makes a person feel uncomfortable. It is God's way of tapping someone on the shoulder, telling him it is time to move outside his comfort zone.

If you have not been made to feel uncomfortable through the teaching of God's Word, this strongly suggests that there is no conviction of sin. But when you are feeling convicted of your sins, past and present, it is a wonderful sign that God is on your case. Accept this attention, for this is the kindness of God; it is His graciousness that leads one to repentance (see Romans 2:4).

Three years was a long time to go without rain; this demonstrates what God does sometimes to get our attention. In this case it was His love for Israel. Was it judgment? Yes. But it was gracious judgment, not simply retributive judgment. God was angry with Ahab's toleration of the prophets of Baal, but He loved Israel and chose it over all other nations.

God's Timing

God had Ahab's attention. The king was now open to what Elijah would propose—namely, a showdown between the true God and the prophets of Baal. This is what Elijah had in mind from the beginning. He knew there was no way this could happen without extreme measures.

Imagine Elijah going to the king's palace before the famine with this request: "Summon the people from all over Israel to meet me on Mount Carmel. And bring the four hundred and fifty prophets of Baal and the four hundred prophets of Asherah, who eat at Jezebel's table" (1 Kings 18:19). This would have been viewed as the most ridiculous, impertinent and insulting request one ever dreamed of! He would have been laughed to scorn, if not killed. But three years without rain worked: Ahab sent word for the people and the prophets to gather on Mount Carmel. Who would have dreamed that Ahab would respond to Elijah's proposition? Timing made the difference. With God all things are possible.

Perhaps you feel you have a message the world needs to hear. Caution: You must first earn the right to deliver that message. If, indeed, what is red-hot in your heart was put there by the Holy Spirit, your time will come. But you have to be willing not only to wait but also to suffer, be misunderstood and be patient as Elijah was. "There is a time for everything, and a season for every activity under heaven: . . . a time to be silent and a time to speak. . . . He has made everything beautiful in its time" (Ecclesiastes 3:1, 7, 11).

> So Ahab sent word throughout all Israel and assembled the prophets on Mount Carmel. Elijah went before the people and said, "How long will you waver between two opinions? If the LORD is God, follow him; but if Baal is God, follow him." But the people said nothing.
>
> 1 Kings 18:20–21

Elijah was now ready to unveil the purpose of the famine: It was to have a platform to address the whole of Israel, especially the false prophets. Ahab could not have known what Elijah also had in mind. Despite the absence of rain he would not have listened to Elijah had he known what Elijah was ultimately planning to do: effectively and completely rid Israel of the false prophets.

But one step at a time in Elijah's strategy. Ahab agreed to order the whole of Israel to assemble on Mount Carmel. Picture this: people coming from all around those parts of Israel to Mount Carmel—the populace, rich and poor, and all 850 false prophets. What a sight and what a crowd! And what a platform that was now given to Elijah! This gathering did not appear in an hour or two, but days later as the word got out: "Everybody get to Mount Carmel, at the king's command."

Once the people were assembled, they were ready to listen to Elijah. He got right to the point: "How long will you waver between two opinions?" Why ask this question? Because the people were sitting on the fence. They could not make up their minds whether to follow the God of Israel or the prophets of Baal.

It is almost unthinkable to imagine the ancient Jews degenerating to the place of being so unspiritual, careless and unbelieving that they would desert the God of their forefathers, but that is the way it was. The prophets of Baal—the god of the demonic world—had elbowed their way in on the people of the covenant of God and completely duped them. The populace did not know which way to turn. There were many who did not want to worship Baal, but they so feared the opinions of people that they became fence-straddlers. The fear of man kept them from worshiping the true God. "Fear of man will prove to be a snare, but whoever trusts in the LORD is kept safe" (Proverbs 29:25).

Are you a fence-straddler? Are you undecided about whether or not Jesus Christ is the only way to God? Jesus said that He is the way, the truth and the life; that no one reaches the Father except through Him (see John 14:6). The earliest message of the Christian Church was this, that there is "no other name under heaven given to men by which we must be saved" (Acts 4:12). I must say kindly to you, if you are a fence-straddler in this matter, it also means you are in the exact same position as those people in ancient Israel who could not make up their minds between worshiping Baal or the true God.

Decision Time

Elijah was within his rights to address the people like this. He was a fellow Israelite who was faithful to the ancient covenant—the covenant they had violated. Furthermore, Elijah was representing the God of the Bible, the true God. Thus, Elijah asked them, "How long will you waver between two opinions? If the Lord is God, follow him; but if Baal is God, follow him." "The LORD" is the Hebrew translation of *Yahweh*, "I AM WHO I AM" (Exodus 3:14).

Elijah's challenge called for a decision. They had to get off the fence. If you are on the fence, you are called to come down on the side of the true God—the God of the Bible, the God who answers prayer, the God who loves us more than we love ourselves, the God who wants only what is best for us. Are you serving this God?

The people were interested in one thing: rain. If Elijah held out hope for rain, they were willing to listen to him. But as Matthew Henry put it, "Deserters must not look for God's favor until they return to their allegiance." John said that we must not love the world or the things that are in the world, because if we love the world the love of the Father is not in us (see 1 John 2:15).

The people in Elijah's day had in common that they were *backsliders*. This is a term that applies to the people of God when they have slipped back, falling into unbelief and idolatry. Jeremiah said that God is married to the backslider (see Jeremiah 3:14), which means that God is committed to His people. If you once came to Christ in saving faith, you are His; if you became a backslider in the meantime, you are still His. Once saved, always saved. God is with you, but He is asking you to get off the fence.

The people's initial reaction to Elijah's message was *silence*: "The people said nothing." The people of Israel, the ordinary people, were gripped by fear. One of the saddest things in all the world is to be motivated by fear. Perfect love casts out fear (see 1 John 4:18). Fear is crippling—psychologically, physically and spiritually—and will keep you from doing what is right. "To thine own self be true," wrote Shakespeare. Fear will keep you from being true to yourself. Coming down off the fence will enable you to be true to yourself—and perhaps become a "troubler" in a godless world.

9

Elijah's Finest Hour

> Then Elijah said to them, "I am the only one of the
> LORD's prophets left, but Baal has four hundred
> and fifty prophets. Get two bulls for us. Let them
> choose one for themselves, and let them cut it into
> pieces and put it on the wood but not set fire to it.
> I will prepare the other bull and put it on the wood
> but not set fire to it. Then you call on the name of
> your god, and I will call on the name of the LORD.
> The god who answers by fire—he is God."
>
> Then all the people said, "What you say is
> good."
>
> 1 Kings 18:22–24

The people—not the prophets of Baal—finally spoke:
"What you say is good." Elijah had made an offer
they could not refuse. They were able also to save
face—that is, not look so shameful for being silent.

The truth is, the people wanted a way out. They knew in their hearts that Elijah was representing the God of their fathers, but they were so backslidden they could not speak—at first. But once Elijah put this proposition to them, they knew they could speak up without being criticized.

In other words, instead of rubbing their noses in it, making them feel bad owing to their fear, he gave them an alternative. All they had to do was to wait and see! I think the prophets of Baal were not keen to accept this proposition, but Elijah had won the people over. They agreed to get off the fence once they saw who the true God was.

It was not the false prophets, then, that Elijah had been addressing up till now. One might think he would want to confront the prophets of Baal and Asherah and rebuke them. No, he was not going to waste time talking to those doomed men. His goal was twofold: (1) to win over the people, and (2) to get rid of the false prophets. So his proposition was put to the people.

Sometimes God does this sort of thing—that is, make propositions with us. He did so with David who sinned by taking a census of the people. God gave him a choice from three possible punishments: (1) three years of famine, (2) three months of fleeing from his enemies or (3) three days of plague (see 2 Samuel 24:13). God knows our frame, remembering that we are dust (see Psalm 103:14). Thus, God makes a deal with a backslidden nation to reveal Himself by answering with fire.

This passage shows how fair and reasonable God is. This does not mean we always understand immediately what He is up to or why He permits some things to happen. But at the end of the day you will always see that the true God is fair.

Elijah Was Not Perfect

This part of the Elijah story also shows that the best of God's servants are not perfect. By any reckoning Elijah stands out as one of the great characters of the Old Testament. And yet here he is before the people on Mount Carmel making a false claim: "I am the only one of the Lord's prophets left."

Wrong.

A stupid comment, a misstatement and a foolish thing to say. Obadiah had just told Elijah a day or two before that there were a hundred prophets being hidden in caves! By taking himself so seriously Elijah showed contempt for Obadiah and the prophets Obadiah was keeping out of harm's way. He fancied he was the only prophet who mattered.

God might have stepped in and ordered Elijah to call the whole thing off! But Scripture tells us that all of God's servants are "jars of clay" (2 Corinthians 4:7)—frail, fallible and feeble at best. God would sort out Elijah later on.

He does that with all of us, not embarrassing us or exposing us every time we make a bad statement. I would hate to think how many unguarded comments I have made in the pulpit over my 58 years of ministry, how many things I have said that were incorrect. God is kind and gracious. He uses imperfect people.

How to Know You Have a Future

God deals only—as on this occasion—with people He loves and for whom there is still a future. The prophets of Baal and Asherah had no future; the people did. Yes, these fence-straddlers had a future. God has declared that His Spirit will not always strive with men (see Genesis 6:3), and this was certainly the case with the false prophets. Their time was up. There comes a time when God says, "Enough is enough." It was *over* for the prophets of Baal, but not for the people.

You may ask, How can we know if we truly have a future and that God has not finished with us yet? I reply that you know because you feel a tugging of the Holy Spirit in your heart. This means you have not become stone-deaf to the Holy Spirit. When you sense that God is trying to get your attention, it is because He *is* indeed trying to get your attention. If, therefore, as you read these lines you can sense that God is calling for you, then be glad and rejoice; you have a future. But *you must not assume you will feel this way tomorrow*. Today is the day of salvation (see 2 Corinthians 6:2). Thank God for any slap on the wrist, any sense of warning. It means you have a future. God always shows a way forward when we are open to His will. Wisdom is knowing the next step forward; God will show you the next thing to do.

Elijah Addresses the False Prophets

Elijah next directed his words to the false prophets. It must have galled these 450 prophets of Baal and 400 prophets of Asherah to have to listen to Elijah. They hated him with unimaginable ire. But they had no choice; the king had commanded them to go to Mount Carmel. Perhaps you would like to say something to people in high places who are ruining the churches and the nations? All you can do is pray as Elijah did to see if God will swear an oath to you, then give you a platform to reach those in power.

Elijah now turned to these fraudulent men. He did not preach to them or prophesy. He did not waste words. He knew they would be out of the picture very soon. He calmly told them to get two bulls, choose one of them, cut their bull into pieces and put it on the wood but not set fire to it. Elijah would do the same.

The deal was this:

> "You call on the name of your god, and I will call on the name of the LORD [Hebrew, *Yahweh*]. The god who answers by fire—he is God. . . . Choose one of the bulls and prepare it first, since there are so many of you. Call on the name of your god, but do not light the fire."
>
> 1 Kings 18:24–25

So they did. It was not natural fire—but supernatural—that Elijah was waiting for.

We are now approaching Elijah's finest hour. It was the high-water mark of his ministry. All his preparation, whether at the Kerith Ravine or in Sidon, anticipated this confrontation with these evil men. This occasion would be regarded afterward with awe, ranking alongside the children of Israel crossing the Red Sea on dry land. It was a triumph not for Elijah himself, however, although he would be held in high esteem; it was vindication of the God of the Bible. God overruled Elijah's frailty. He does this, using imperfect servants, so He will get the glory.

Elijah's proposing was daring, but decisive: to see which god would answer by fire. This was a scary thing to suggest! What if no fire came? How would Elijah feel—and how would it affect his credibility? How did he know he could get away with this? Do you think he was biting his lip as he proposed this to the prophets of Baal?

Here is our answer: Elijah had God's *oath*. He knew he was safe to challenge the false prophets as he did. What is more, he was fearless. This means he was not merely courageous, but calm, without fear. He had no doubt that God would come through and answer by fire. But more than that, the people considered this proposition to be a fair one. If the God of their fathers was indeed God Almighty and Creator, His showing up would remove all doubt as to whether or not the prophets of Baal were right. Elijah made a proposition that forced the prophets of Baal to comply.

Seeking the True God

The people had been hoodwinked by these false prophets for a long, long time. The people were intimidated, they were in fear—but they were far from convinced that Baal was God. What relief it was to them when Elijah put forth the proposition that the God who answered by fire was the true God! "What you say is good," they responded. They were rooting for Elijah.

I believe there are countless millions all over the world who want to see an undoubted display of the God of the Bible. I refer to people in all religions—Buddhism, Islam, Shintoism, Hinduism and even a Christianity that has denied the Scriptures and the power of God. These people are in fear. They feel they have no choice but to accept things as they are. Nothing would thrill them more than to see a demonstration in power of the undiluted Gospel of Jesus Christ. Elijah's proposition gave them sweet relief: "What you say is good."

And yet it would have seemed more reasonable had Elijah said, "The God who answers by *rain* is the true God." They needed rain. Fire was the last thing they needed; the landscape was already brittle and vulnerable to the slightest spark.

But think about it: Have you known a time when the last thing you thought you needed was what you got? "'My thoughts are not your thoughts, neither are your ways my ways,' declares the LORD" (Isaiah 55:8). God loves to surprise us with His plans. He chooses the foolish things of the world to confound the wise (see 1 Corinthians 1:27). The last thing anybody could have dreamed of was that the Son of God should die on a cross to save us from our sins!

When Elijah said, "The god who answers by fire—he is God," it assumed that God is *alive*. Elijah initially approached Ahab with the oath, "As the LORD, the God of Israel, *lives* . . ." (1 Kings 17:1, emphasis added). The fence-straddlers had forgotten this—that the true God is alive. This means He can do *anything*. It gave the people a great sense of anticipation. Nothing is more uplifting than having genuine expectancy that something good is going to happen. That is what Elijah was promising these people.

God's Unusual Plan

All that I am saying in this chapter assumes that God answers prayer. "May the LORD answer you when you are in distress," said David. "May he give you the desire of your heart and make all your plans succeed" (Psalm 20:1, 4). All that Elijah was doing was based on his belief that God answers prayer. Remember: It was he who had prayed that it would not rain. Prayer is the greatest fringe benefit of being a Christian. I cannot imagine life without prayer. I would not pray, however, if I thought I was not speaking to the living God who answers my prayers.

But Elijah was praying for *fire*. Why?

For one thing, there was a long connection between God's ancient people and fire. Moses witnessed the burning bush that was not consumed (see Exodus 3:2). When the Lord descended on Mount Sinai, "smoke billowed up from it like smoke from a furnace" (Exodus 19:18). At the ancient Tent of Meeting, when the glory of the Lord appeared to all the people, "[f]ire came out from the presence of the LORD and consumed the burnt offering" (Leviticus 9:23–24).

By saying, "The God who answers by fire—he is God," Elijah found an entry point into the hearts of the Israelites. This offering of a bull in pieces would have reminded them specifically of that ancient burnt offering at the Tent of Meeting that was consumed by the fire of God. They would have thought, *That is the God we are supposed to believe in.*

There are two kinds of fire: natural fire, that which goes up, and supernatural fire, that which comes down. The fire that Elijah was anticipating was supernatural fire—fire that comes down, fire for which there is no natural explanation. This was seen on the day of Pentecost. After the blowing of a violent wind from heaven the people saw "what seemed to be tongues of fire that separated and came to rest on each of them" (Acts 2:3). Remember, as well, that John the Baptist said Jesus would baptize "with the Holy Spirit and with fire" (Matthew 3:11).

Fire, then, not rain, was next on God's agenda. All who did not love the true God would be exposed; the fire would bring this to light. It was showdown time.

Elijah's Sense of Humor

We have referred to the oath given to Elijah by God: infallible assurance. This is what made Elijah calm. So at peace with himself was Elijah at this moment, that his sense of humor emerged. It is one of the most hilarious episodes in all of Holy Writ:

So they took the bull given them and prepared it. Then they called on the name of Baal from morning till noon. "O Baal, answer us!" they shouted. But there was no response; no one answered. And they danced around the altar they had made.

At noon Elijah began to taunt them. "Shout louder!" he said. "Surely he is a god! Perhaps he is deep in thought, or busy, or traveling. Maybe he is sleeping and must be awakened." So they shouted louder and slashed themselves with swords and spears, as was their custom, until their blood flowed. Midday passed, and they continued their frantic prophesying until the time for the evening sacrifice. But there was no response, no one answered, no one paid attention.

1 Kings 18:26–29

Do you have a sense of humor? You might have thought that this moment was too sacred to be funny. Some think that laughter has no place in church. The great Charles Spurgeon was criticized for his humor in the pulpit. His reply was, "If you only knew how much I held back!" I am sure that Jesus made the common people, who heard Him gladly, laugh at times. Jesus sometimes poked fun at the Pharisees—their sounding a trumpet whenever they gave to the poor (see Matthew 6:1–8), or making "their phylacteries wide and the tassels on their garments long"—doing everything "for men to see" (Matthew 23:5).

Elijah began to taunt the prophets of Baal who were having difficulty getting Baal to reply. "O Baal, answer us!" they shouted.

"Shout louder!" Elijah said to them. "Perhaps he is deep in thought or busy or traveling [Hebrew, *sitting on the toilet*]. Maybe he is sleeping and must be awakened." This shows how calm and at ease Elijah was. No biting of his nails. No anxiety. He was enjoying every minute of this. Martin

Luther used to say that the devil cannot stand ridicule. That is precisely what Elijah was doing here.

Common sense would have led these prophets of Baal to give up, but the demonic was now in full sway: "They shouted louder and slashed themselves with swords and spears, as was their custom, until the blood flowed." Idolatry led to self-abuse; it always does. It was getting later—moving into the afternoon—and they continued "their frantic prophesying. . . . But there was no response, no one answered, no one paid attention."

It is as though Elijah said to them, "Are you finished?" They were finished.

10

The Fire of God

Then Elijah said to all the people, "Come here to me." They came to him, and he repaired the altar of the Lord, which was in ruins. Elijah took twelve stones, one for each of the tribes descended from Jacob, to whom the word of the Lord had come, saying, "Your name shall be Israel." With the stones he built an altar in the name of the Lord, and he dug a trench around it large enough to hold two seahs of seed. He arranged the wood, cut the bull into pieces and laid it on the wood. Then he said to them, "Fill four large jars with water and pour it on the offering and on the wood."

"Do it again," he said, and they did it again.

"Do it a third time," he ordered, and they did it the third time. The water ran down around the altar and even filled the trench.

1 Kings 18:30–35

Elijah now turned from the false prophets to the people. They were the ones he was determined to win over. The prophets of Baal, humiliated, failed in their efforts to get Baal to answer.

"Come to me," Elijah said to the people. They came to him. The next thing he did was to repair the altar of the Lord, which was in ruins. The prophets of Baal had no interest in their history or blessed heritage. The covenant of God meant nothing to them.

"Come to me," said Elijah. Please note that he did not rush into calling upon God to send fire. Elijah was in no hurry. He wanted to make an important statement by what he did before he prayed.

"Come to me." Elijah wanted the people to see firsthand what he was doing. He showed reverence for the altar of the Lord. Not only did the altar mean nothing to the prophets of Baal, but God's people had not been taught what the altar represented. Furthermore, it needed to be repaired because the followers of Baal had treated it with contempt.

The reference to the twelve tribes was to remind the people of their glorious heritage. They were not like any other nation: They were God's covenant people; they were God's treasure. They had a sacred history, going back to Moses and the patriarchs—Abraham, Isaac and Jacob.

Elijah called for a bull for the sole purpose of shedding blood. From ancient times, shedding the blood of an animal was central to the sacrificial system. The sacrificial system was given to Moses from God to show Israel's sin and the need for atonement. Elijah, therefore, wanted to demonstrate the seriousness of all that he was doing. For this reason he did not hastily and hurriedly pray for the fire to fall; he wanted first to show deference to the foundations of the Mosaic Law.

The shedding of blood must come before the descent of fire. Though no one would have grasped it at the time, this event was also prophetic, pointing to the future shedding of the blood of their Messiah centuries later—when Jesus died on the cross—which was followed by the fire of Pentecost.

With the stones, then, Elijah built an altar in the name of the Lord, tying this event to their historic past, which the worshipers of Baal and the people had lost sight of. Elijah the prophet had now become Elijah the teacher. Never had solid teaching been so needed! God raised up this man who was acquainted not only with the power of God, but also the Scriptures. Jesus later accused the Sadducees of knowing neither the Scriptures nor the power of God (see Matthew 22:29). Elijah knew both.

The next thing Elijah did was to ensure that nobody could say it was natural fire on display. He dug a large trench, arranged the wood, cut the bull into pieces and laid it on the wood. Although water was exceedingly scarce and very, very precious, Elijah ordered that a lot of water—four large jars—be poured onto the pieces of bull—the "offering"—and the wood. That having been done, Elijah ordered, "Do it again." They did. If that were not enough, Elijah commanded them, "Do it a third time." By now there was so much water that it ran down around the altar and even filled the trench.

Nowadays, "miracles" often have a natural explanation. I have no problem with doctors, surgery, medicine or good vitamins. And I believe God heals through these things. But although we rightly give God the glory when we are healed through modern medicine, the truth is, there is also the obvious natural explanation—namely, the same modern medicine. But when there is no medicine, no doctor, no surgery— nothing but God who steps in and heals—one has to say that there was no natural explanation for the miracle. That is what Elijah did; he made sure that nobody could say there was a natural explanation to the fire coming down.

> At the time of sacrifice, the prophet Elijah stepped forward and prayed: "O LORD, God of Abraham, Isaac and Israel, let it be known today that you are God in Israel and that I am your servant and have done all these things at your command. Answer me, O LORD, answer me, so these people will know that you, O LORD, are God, and that you are turning their hearts back again."
>
> 1 Kings 18:36–37

It was now time to pray—that is, it was Elijah's turn. It was a simple prayer, a brief prayer. Jesus said we are not heard for our "many words" (Matthew 6:7). We do not know if Elijah kneeled, sat or stood. What we do know is that there was no frantic shouting. The nearest he came to repetition was when he said, "Answer me, O Lord, answer me." Elijah wanted vindication of the true God—"O Lord . . . let it be known today that You are God in Israel." Elijah spoke a few words to clarify that he was not doing this because it was his own idea. Neither was there a personal grudge or private vendetta behind Elijah's actions. He stated, "I am Your servant and have done all these things at Your command." The people needed to see this for themselves.

It is so comforting and reassuring when we know that we are doing things under *God's* command. When I preach or write I need to know it is *God's* Word I am teaching—not my silly point of view—and that the purity of His Word is at stake. Elijah thus put his own integrity and teaching on the line: If God showed up it meant double vindication—for God and Elijah. If God did not show up, it meant that Elijah was no more to be believed than the prophets of Baal. Elijah's sole burden was for the good of the people: "that you are turning their hearts back again." It meant true revival—when God's people are awakened and are given hearts that long to do His will.

> Then the fire of the LORD fell and burned up the sacrifice, the wood, the stones and the soil, and also licked up the water in the trench. When all the people saw this, they fell prostrate and cried, "The LORD—he is God! The LORD—he is God!"
>
> 1 Kings 18:38–39

What a sight it must have been! I would love to have been there. I cannot imagine fire falling—it always rises. But this was not natural fire; it was supernatural. Instead of the rain they wanted, they got the fire they needed. They needed to see that the God of Israel was behind the famine—to get their attention—and that this was the God of Abraham, Isaac and Jacob—to demonstrate who was the true God. Fire "falling." Perhaps it was like poured water except that it was supernatural fire. I reckon God will let us see a DVD replay when we get to heaven.

We do not know how much of an interval there was between Elijah's prayer and the fire falling. I suppose the people were quiet. They waited. They looked up. Was it in seconds? A minute or two? All we know is, after Elijah prayed there came a most spectacular sight from heaven: Fire, supernatural fire, fell on the sacrifice—burning it up and even sucking out all the water in the trench. Never before had there been a moment like it.

No faith was needed to be convinced that God was at work. The people saw this and fell prostrate. True faith is believing without seeing (see Hebrews 11:1). The people believed, yes, but it was *seeing*—which means that faith was not needed to accept all that happened. That is the way it is when God vindicates Himself. You do not need faith then. It is the way it will be at Jesus' Second Coming: "Look, he is coming with clouds, and every eye will see him, even those who pierced him; and all the peoples of the earth will mourn because of him. So shall it be! Amen" (Revelation 1:7). The fire falling on the sacrifice was visible, requiring no faith. The visible fire burned up the sacrifice, the wood, the stones and even licked up the water in the trench.

Fire falling, as it did on Mount Carmel, was unusual; indeed, it was unique. God could do this all the time, but for some reason He did it only in Elijah's day. Why then and not at other times when Israel's spiritual state was so terrible? You tell me. But it happened then, and it would be talked about for generations—even centuries. It is the reason Elijah appeared with Moses when Jesus was transfigured (see Matthew 17:3). The transfiguration of Jesus itself was also unique; it never happened again. Apocalyptic events like these are given to us as proof of what it will be like when God displays His glory to the whole world, when every knee shall bow and every tongue confess that Jesus Christ is Lord to the glory of God the Father (see Philippians 2:9–11).

More Work to Do

But Elijah's mission on Mount Carmel was not finished. He might have basked in a moment of ecstasy and glory, enjoying seeing the people prostrate, worshiping, shouting, "The Lord—He is God!" But that was not to be. Had Elijah stopped there, the prophets of Baal would have been back in a very short period of time to undo the good he had done.

Elijah knew this and, consequently, gave further orders to the people.

> Then Elijah commanded them, "Seize the prophets of Baal. Don't let anyone get away!" They seized them, and Elijah had them brought down to the Kishon Valley and slaughtered there.
>
> 1 Kings 18:40

This verse further shows that those who do not worship the true God will eventually be found out—and punished. God says:

> "If you had responded to my rebuke, I would have poured out my heart to you. . . . But since you rejected me when I called and no one gave heed when I stretched out my hand, since you ignored all my advice and would not accept my rebuke, I in turn will laugh at your disaster; I will mock when calamity overtakes you—when calamity overtakes you like a storm, when disaster sweeps over you like a whirlwind, when distress and trouble overwhelm you."
>
> Proverbs 1:23–27

This is an example of what it will be like on the Last Day, when God clears His name and the wicked are consigned to "outer darkness: there shall be weeping and gnashing of teeth" (Matthew 8:12, KJV).

Elijah's work on Mount Carmel, in other words, was far from over. The task now was to rid Israel of these false prophets, and the people—newly turned back to God—acted quickly on Elijah's directive to slaughter them.

It was not enough for the fire to fall: "Revival came—and went" could describe some blessings of the Holy Spirit on the Church. Whereas no time of renewal should be underestimated, it happens all too often that the devil gets into a church soon afterward. This is partly because the people are content merely to see the "fire fall," as it were, and be swept along in ecstatic worship. It is historical fact that John Wesley was sovereignly used of God following the spectacular successes of his friend and fellow clergyman George Whitefield. Whitefield preached, and moved on. Wesley, using his superb organizational skills, directed their converts into order and structure. The Methodist Church, founded principally by Wesley, along with Whitefield and Charles Wesley, is a great legacy showing Wesley's organizational ability to keep converts on the right track.

Another way of describing this portion of Elijah's effective ministry is follow-up—a vital step for those who make a profession of faith. It is true that this does not happen in every instance—even when there is genuine conversion. That is the case with the Ethiopian eunuch who was converted by Philip while riding in his carriage along a desert road. Philip led the eunuch to Christ, then was carried away by the Spirit, apparently leaving this Ethiopian to sort out things on his own (see Acts 8:39). But that is exceptional. Most converts need attentive follow-up. They need to be told to read their Bibles every day—as well as pray daily, witness for Christ daily, learn to recognize and turn away from temptation, resist the devil and find a church where Christ is truly honored and the Bible is faithfully preached.

We have witnessed Elijah's finest hour, the high-water mark of his ministry. But God had more work for him to do; indeed, his most important work in a sense: to bring rain back to Israel.

11

The Sound of Rain

And Elijah said to Ahab, "Go, eat and drink, for there is the sound of a heavy rain." So Ahab went off to eat and drink, but Elijah climbed to the top of Carmel, bent down to the ground and put his face between his knees.

1 Kings 18:41–42

Have you ever smelled rain—having needed it so much—just before it rained? It takes me back to my childhood in the hills of Kentucky. We lived on Hilton Avenue, at the bottom of a hill. We knew it would rain when the wind began to blow all of a sudden, bringing with it an indescribable fragrance. Then we could actually hear it coming as it fell first on the hill in front of our house. The wind, the smell and the sound let us know that rain was at hand. To me the smell of rain is one of life's most exhilarating experiences.

Elijah did not say anything to Ahab about the smell of rain but referred, rather, to the *sound* of "heavy" rain. Elijah could hear rain—prophetically, in the Spirit—even though rain had not yet come. King Ahab was the next person to know this.

Elijah then decided to climb to the very top of Mount Carmel to pray. Mount Carmel is a few miles west of the modern city of Haifa. I have stood on the top of that mountain, presumably where Elijah prayed. You can see the Mediterranean Sea to the west and picture that cloud about the size of a man's hand, as we will see below.

But if Elijah could hear rain, why did he need to pray for rain? John Wesley said that God does nothing but in answer to prayer. God dignifies us by letting us participate in the next thing on His agenda. He sometimes stirs us to pray; we sometimes feel it is our idea and begin pleading with Him to work. God loves to do this, this being one of His ways. Elijah was experiencing this. James referred to this moment, when Elijah prayed a second time, "and the heavens gave rain, and the earth produced its crops" (James 5:18).

When God reveals something prophetically, He is bringing into the present moment what has not yet transpired. God said to Joshua, "I have delivered Jericho into your hands, along with its king and its fighting men" (Joshua 6:2). Joshua still had to circle Jericho seven times before the walls came down, but with God the walls had already fallen. God called Gideon a "mighty warrior" when, in fact, Gideon was by nature a weak man (see Judges 6:12). God imputed strength to Gideon because that is the way God saw him. This is the same way we are justified: God imputes to us righteousness. When we rely on His grace, God declares us righteous even when we do not feel the slightest bit righteous or have done any good works (see Romans 5:18–21). So, too, with Elijah and rain; Elijah heard the sound of rain when it had not yet rained a drop.

Elijah's prophetic word persuaded Ahab. The king went off to eat and drink, although food was being rationed and water was scarce. Ahab believed this time. The first time Elijah gave a negative word, that there would be neither dew nor rain, Ahab did not believe a word of it. He saw Elijah only as a troubler in Israel. But the fire falling on Mount Carmel opened Ahab's eyes. And now Elijah's forecast of rain meant that everything was changing—so you, Ahab, can eat and drink all you like. And he did just that.

We now see Elijah "bent to the ground" with his face between his knees. It is difficult to know whether Elijah was sitting or kneeling. Probably kneeling as kneeling suggests greater reverence and a feeling of the need of mercy. Posture in prayer is not a big issue to God. There is a biblical basis for any posture you can imagine—standing, sitting, kneeling, walking or lying flat on your back or face. In any case, Elijah had the responsibility to make good what he had told Ahab. Ahab believed, but Elijah now sought the Lord to answer.

Things were not as forthcoming as he might have thought. Whether Elijah was sitting or kneeling with his face between his knees, the picture suggests his feeling of helplessness. The rain had not come yet. What does a prophet do when he has made a forecast? He prays. He pleads. He waits. He does not arrogantly snap his fingers as if by magic he can make things happen. No, a true prophet is helpless before God and grateful when God steps in. "'Go and look toward the sea,' he told his servant. And he went up and looked. 'There is nothing there,' he said. Seven times Elijah said, 'Go back'" (1 Kings 18:43).

This is the first reference to Elijah having a servant. Whether this servant had been with him all the time up to now is not known, but it is likely. While Elijah prayed, the servant watched. Having been told to "look toward the sea," the servant reported that there was "nothing there." This must have been disappointing to Elijah, but it shows that God does not always jump to our request as soon as we ask Him. Even when Elijah prays! God is sovereign, and we should always begin any praying by asking first for mercy. You ask for mercy, then you find grace (see Hebrews 4:16). The great prophet Elijah had to keep praying. "Seven times Elijah said, 'Go back.'"

Jesus said, "Ask and it will be given to you; seek and you will find; knock and the door will be opened to you" (Matthew 7:7). The Greek tense in these verbs shows that we ask but *keep on asking*; we seek but *keep on seeking*; we knock and *keep on knocking*. Jesus taught that we should never, never, never give up when it comes to prayer (see Luke 18:1). I cannot begin to describe how much this verse and this concept mean to me. There are items on my prayer list that I was asking and praying about years ago. I refuse to give up. Seven times Elijah said his servant, "Go back." Keep watching. God is never too early, never too late, but always just on time. "The seventh time the servant reported, 'A cloud as small as a man's hand is rising from the sea'" (1 Kings 18:44).

With all of us there comes a time when we need to see as well as believe; we need the objective proof as well as having the inner testimony of the Spirit. Elijah heard rain—in the Spirit. But this kind of hearing could not go on indefinitely when you just told the king to eat and drink because rain is on the way. Elijah needed to see something *happening*. The moment the servant reported—and the report did not seem like much, noting that he saw "a cloud as small as a man's hand"—Elijah was set. He knew that God was stepping in. It was the first cloud anybody in that area had seen in three years. Elijah knew that the sound of rain was not a fanciful hope; rain, beautiful, needed and welcomed rain was seconds away. It was arguably the happiest moment in Elijah's life.

The cloud about the size of a man's hand was to Elijah like God's oath. There was no need to keep praying; God had answered. When God swears an oath, it means an infallible, absolute, definite and unconditional assurance of God showing up and answering our prayer. No room for doubting is left. The struggle is over. Elijah was now ready to leave Mount Carmel. "So Elijah said, 'Go and tell Ahab, "Hitch up your chariot and go down before the rain stops you"'" (1 Kings 18:44).

Both Elijah and the king were still on Mount Carmel. They needed to move quickly: Heavy rain was on the way. It would take several minutes to get down to the bottom of this mountain. They could waste no time.

There are times when God moves slowly. Oh, so slowly! Three years of waiting for rain was a long time. But there are times when He comes suddenly. And—oh, so suddenly!—as when "[s]uddenly a great company of the heavenly host appeared with the angel" to the shepherds to announce Jesus' birth (Luke 2:13). Or as when "[s]uddenly a sound like the blowing of a violent wind came from heaven" on the day of Pentecost (Acts 2:2). "Then suddenly the Lord you are seeking will come to his temple" (Malachi 3:1). Now things were happening so fast that Ahab was told to get moving before the rain kept him stuck on Mount Carmel! No rain had yet fallen, but it was coming.

> Meanwhile, the sky grew black with clouds, the wind rose, a heavy rain came on and Ahab rode off to Jezreel. The power

of the LORD came upon Elijah and, tucking his cloak into his belt, he ran ahead of Ahab all the way to Jezreel.

1 Kings 18:45–46

At long last there was objective evidence that rain was on the way. A sky growing black with clouds must have been the most welcome, satisfying and beautiful sight anybody could remember. The sight of the black clouds! The feel of the wind and the smell of rain! The long nightmare was over. An end of a tortuous era. God was at work. All because He loves with a jealous love, which He bestowed on Israel alone.

There is one more thing to be noted in this story—Elijah's running. We are told that the "power of the Lord" came upon Elijah, and that he ran ahead of Ahab all the way to Jezreel. This is quite extraordinary. First, Elijah's speed: He ran ahead of Ahab's chariot that was empowered by one or more horses. Second, the distance: Elijah ran at least twenty miles or more. The best runner in the world could not match that. The only explanation is the power of the Lord.

Why this power to run? Why did he need to run ahead of the king all the way to Jezreel? For two reasons. First, Elijah's running demonstrates the sort of thing that is possible by the power of the Holy Spirit. Time is God's domain. He can make things happen for which there is no natural explanation. He can use angels to accomplish travel and shorten distances (so it would seem). This final scenario of Elijah's finest hour simply shows once more that God can, indeed, do anything.

Second, which may be the main reason for Elijah getting to Jezreel ahead of Ahab, it kept Jezebel from grabbing Elijah before he got away. We are told in the next verse (see 1 Kings 19:1) that Ahab told Jezebel how Elijah had killed the prophets of Baal with the sword. Jezebel vowed to kill Elijah. Because Elijah got there first, she was not able to find him.

God, therefore, preserved Elijah. Although he would never again reach the spectacular height of seeing the fire of God consume a sacrifice on Mount Carmel, it is equally true that God was not finished with him yet. God not only uses us for His glory, but cares about us as His children.

12

Running Scared

Now Ahab told Jezebel everything Elijah had done and how he had killed all the prophets with the sword. So Jezebel sent a messenger to Elijah to say, "May the gods deal with me, be it ever so severely, if by this time tomorrow I do not make your life like one of them." Elijah was afraid and ran for his life. When he came to Beersheba in Judah, he left his servant there, while he himself went a day's journey into the desert.

1 Kings 19:1–4

Jonathan Edwards said that when the Church is revived, so is the devil. What Elijah accomplished was an immense encouragement to the people of Israel. They were now united against the forces of evil. When Jezebel heard from Ahab what had happened on Mount Carmel, she vowed to get revenge. This is exactly the way the devil is, and how he influences those he has possessed. When God is mightily at work, the devil will be right there to get revenge and do all he can do to destroy the work of God—or demoralize his servants. Queen Jezebel was in the grip of Satan.

Enter Queen Jezebel

Ahab told Jezebel everything Elijah had done—which means she learned of the fire falling supernaturally when Elijah prayed. That in itself should have mellowed Jezebel and given her pause. You would think that with such undoubted supernatural manifestation of *Yahweh* she would humble herself and say, "I, too, want to be on the side of the God of Israel." But, no. She dug in her heels and vowed revenge to kill the true prophet of God.

It was the same way with the Jews in Jesus' day. You would think that the many miracles of Jesus, plus His raising Lazarus from the dead, would win everybody over. Surely these events proved that Jesus was all He claimed to be, but the Sanhedrin plotted immediately after the Lazarus miracle to kill Jesus (see John 11:47). The "god of this age has blinded the minds of unbelievers" (2 Corinthians 4:4), this being the state into which all people are born. In some cases Satan gets an even greater grip, this being the case with Jezebel—one of the most wicked human beings in all history.

I have spoken of the *oath* in this book. You will recall that Elijah confronted Ahab initially with this oath: "As the LORD, the God of Israel, lives, whom I serve, there will be neither dew nor rain in the next few years except at my word" (1 Kings 17:1). That was stated in the power of the Holy Spirit. Jezebel now did the same thing—except her oath was powered by her own strength: "May the gods deal with me, be it ever so severely, if by this time tomorrow I do not make your life like one of them." Elijah had nothing to worry about; his oath was given in the power of the Holy Spirit. He had warrant from the God of Israel to say what he had said. The rest was up to God. But when Jezebel swore an oath, it was up to her to get revenge.

Jesus told us not to swear at all "either by heaven, for it is God's throne; or by the earth, for it is his footstool; or by Jerusalem, for it is the city of the Great King" (Matthew 5:34–35). In the Old Testament oaths were allowed and even encouraged—but the person had better keep that oath. "It is better not to vow than to make a vow and not fulfill it" (Ecclesiastes 5:5). Jezebel swore by her gods, but neither they nor she had the power to destroy Elijah.

People today who bring the name of the Lord into their conversations—such as, "The Lord told me this"—should be very, very careful. First, bringing in the Lord's name is tantamount to swearing an oath. Second, they do it not to make God look good, but themselves. In Jezebel's case she was beside herself with rage. She lost her temper. She was not able to fulfill her vow, but this would not matter. She was under Satan's power.

Two Elijahs?

Now see the contrast between the Elijah *of* Mount Carmel and the Elijah *after* Mount Carmel. Note the contrast between the Elijah who ran ahead of Ahab by the power of the Lord, and the Elijah who now "ran for his life" when he panicked. How could this happen? Had God deserted Elijah? What happened to that power, that courage, that fearlessness? Was it the same man? Yes. But it was Elijah as he would be in his own strength.

When Elijah received Jezebel's message, he was seized with fear. From that moment he was running scared. You would not have dreamed that Elijah the man of God could turn out to be merely Elijah the man. "Just like us," said James (5:17). Elijah's finest hour was now eclipsed by his worst moment. Hours before he was elated and running to Jezreel with uncanny energy. Now he was fearful, weak, hurt and depressed.

Dr. James Dobson has observed shrewdly that many ministers think the devil is attacking them on Mondays to get vengeance for Sunday's hard work. It is probably not that, says Dr. Dobson: It is more likely their being depleted of adrenaline. We ministers thrive on Sundays by the power of the Spirit, yes; but adrenaline also kicks in. By Monday morning that adrenaline is gone. We need a day to recover. And while recovering we are often weak, irritable, vulnerable to any kind of onslaught or criticism. We are like Elijah running from Jezebel. The loss of adrenaline, plus being left to himself for a while, is part of the explanation for Elijah's running scared.

We are all like that. As long as the anointing of the Spirit is resting on us, there is a sense of God, the presence of the mind of the Spirit, the fruits of the Holy Spirit and a feeling of well-being. If we are not careful we begin to think we have "arrived"—that we are set and will forever have victory over the world, the flesh and the devil. Whoa! Sorry, but sooner rather than later we will find ourselves blushing over our hasty good impression of ourselves. I know what it is to walk down from that lofty pulpit at Westminster Chapel having preached so well that I say to myself, *Now I know how to preach! The crowds will be doubled next week.* Wrong! The following week would bring the same crowd—sometimes smaller—but my preaching would be utterly pitiful. God knows how we need to be humbled. As we have seen, Elijah already had a problem taking himself too seriously. Now more than ever would he need to be dealt with by a loving heavenly Father.

As far as I can tell Elijah would never again experience all that he had experienced on Mount Carmel. Was God finished with him? Now that God had gotten what was needed through Elijah, would He cast this prophet to one side? No. This is so encouraging. God loves us as men and women—not as sovereign vessels that do great exploits for Him. We all need to be cared for—and loved—right to the day of our going Home, perhaps long after we are of much use to Him.

Frail Humanity

So what was next for Elijah? He had a mega triumph on Mount Carmel. Would God say, "Congratulations!"? Would He send a thousand angels to minister to Elijah? Would Elijah be welcomed in the king's palace? No. There were no congratulations from the king or queen—or from God. Jesus said in one of His parables that the master of the house does not bother to thank the servant because he did what he was told to do. "So you also, when you have done everything you were told to do, should say, 'We are unworthy servants; we have only done our duty'" (Luke 17:9–10).

It was not unlike Martin Luther's finest hour. Luther stood before the hierarchy in Wittenberg, Germany, and uttered those famous words: "Here I stand. I can do no other. God help me. Amen." Those words were soon heard throughout Europe. Did the angels come to Luther and say, "Congratulations!"? Luther—often fighting depression—had to be hid in Wartburg Castle for a year or two just to stay alive. No apparent thanks from God.

John the Baptist was seen as Elijah's sort of "second coming." Malachi's final word in the Old Testament was: "I will
send you the prophet Elijah before that great and dreadful
day of the LORD comes"(Malachi 4:5). The angel Gabriel
prophesied to Zechariah that his son, John, would go before
the Lord "in the spirit and power of Elijah" (Luke 1:17).
Jesus said that John the Baptist was "the Elijah who was to
come" (Matthew 11:14). And, yet, John the Baptist had his
weak moment, too. He who spoke with such authority and
certainty, proclaiming Jesus as the "Lamb of God" (John 1:36)
and the "one who comes from above" (John 3:31), apparently
doubted his own message later on. He sent a surprising question to Jesus, "Are you the one who was to come, or should
we expect someone else?" (Matthew 11:3).

The truth is, apart from the gracious anointing of the
Holy Spirit we are all weak, fragile, mortal and pitiful. It is
said of King Hezekiah that the Lord "left him to test him
and to know everything that was in his heart" (2 Chronicles
32:31). In his final days Hezekiah, proved himself to be less
than heroic (see Isaiah 39:5–8). We are all children of dust.
The godliest of men are men at best.

Leaving Jezreel, Elijah headed for Beersheba, in the southern part of Israel. We note that his servant remained there
while Elijah went farther into the desert. This time Elijah was
clearly by himself. A person's true character often emerges
when he or she is utterly alone.

Elijah's Further Preparation

God's preparation varies from person to person. There is no
stereotypical preparation for all; God deals with all of us as
individuals—one at a time. Sometimes God thrusts a person

right into ministry without much preparation—as he did the young Saul of Tarsus (see Acts 9:20–22). But the same Saul was soon whisked away to Arabia and other places before his apostolic ministry truly began (see Galatians 1:17).

Dr. Martyn Lloyd-Jones used to say to me, "The worst thing that can happen to a man is to succeed before he is ready." God saw to it that Saul did not succeed before he was ready. To ensure that Saul—who became the great apostle Paul—did not take himself too seriously, God also sent the "thorn in the flesh." This, said Paul, was to keep him from being "conceited" (2 Corinthians 12:7) or "exalted above measure" (KJV).

To put it another way, God can begin using a person immediately without a lot of preparation, but that person will need to be prepared at some stage. We all need it. I myself began preaching within a week of feeling "called to preach." Within three months I was the pastor of a church in Palmer, Tennessee—a ministry with very little preparation that lasted some fourteen months. But my major preparation lay in the future, the years spent selling vacuum cleaners door to door.

In any case, Elijah had huge success at Mount Carmel. You could *almost* wonder if he succeeded before he was ready in that he was taking himself very seriously before the people (remember his line: "I am the only one left")—a malady in Elijah that God would deal with later on. In other words, the lack of preparation does not prohibit God's using us. If we have a larger ministry down the road, we will sooner or later need more preparation—even if we have apparent success early on. This is what would be happening to Elijah under the broom tree, as we will see below.

This part of Elijah's life is yet another example of how God uses ordinary people. Those in biblical history and

Church history are often made "larger than life," whether it is Abraham, Moses, Elijah, St. Augustine, Luther or Calvin. Whereas biographers tend to gloss over their heroes' faults, the Bible does not do this. If we knew as much about some of our heroes as we do, say, about Moses, David or Elijah, we might become a bit disillusioned. Elijah—a most extraordinary prophet—was an ordinary man.

Attack Mode

While a depletion of adrenaline on any given Monday morning can leave us feeling weak and expose our human frailties all too well, it is certainly possible that the devil will use this time to take advantage of us.

One of King David's most glorious moments was when he danced before the Ark of the Lord, after he had finally succeeded in bringing the Ark to Jerusalem. He was elated; it seemed too good to be true. "David, wearing a linen ephod, danced before the LORD with all his might, while he and the entire house of Israel brought up the ark of the LORD with shouts and the sound of trumpets" (2 Samuel 6:14–15).

David had done this for one reason: to honor and glorify God. But his own wife Michal "despised him in her heart" for his excitement (verse 16). As soon as he got home, Michal brought him right down: "How the king of Israel has distinguished himself today, disrobing in the sight of the slave girls of his servants as any vulgar fellow would!" (verse 20).

The devil does not want us to have joy. He will attack us when we are in good form and on top. "Be self-controlled and alert. Your enemy the devil prowls around like a roaring lion looking for someone to devour" (1 Peter 5:8). What is our proper response? "Resist him, standing firm in the faith" (verse 9).

Spiritual Warfare: Stand

One of the most important lessons in spiritual warfare is that it is mainly and essentially *defensive*. We must never— ever—go looking for a fight with the devil. Never pick a fight with him. He will defeat you if you do this. You do not have God's promise of protection when you go out on your own to initiate a fight with Satan. The greatest New Testament passage on spiritual warfare is Ephesians 6:10–18. Paul tells us what to do when the devil attacks: *stand*.

Four times in this passage Paul uses the word *stand*. This is defensive warfare. All we need do when Satan attacks is to stand. Don't run. Don't go backward. Don't trip. Don't even walk. Just stand. Standing against a satanic attack is great progress. Elijah ran.

When we, like Elijah, miss the mark in these things, we have some measure of help in the fact that Satan always overreaches himself. He always miscalculates. Jezebel's threat gave Elijah time. As we have seen, God was not finished with Elijah; there were more plans for him and he would need further preparation. The devil does not know the future; he guesses at best. The biggest surprise to him was Jesus' death on the cross. Satan saw that as his personal victory, but the devil overreached himself when he masterminded the crucifixion of Jesus. He could not have known it was actually God's way to save the world (see Acts 2:23; 4:28). "None of the rulers of this age understood it, for if they had, they would not have crucified the Lord of glory" (1 Corinthians 2:8).

The attack on Elijah, then, orchestrated by Satan through Jezebel, would be a significant part of Elijah's further preparation. The next phase of Elijah's ministry would not be as high profile or spectacular as the fire falling on Mount Carmel, but it was equally precious for him—*and also for us*. What Elijah was to learn under the broom tree became a priceless insight into God's ways for all the Church. Elijah was about to discover new and fresh ways of God.

13

Elijah Gets Depressed

> He came to a broom tree, sat down under it and
> prayed that he might die. "I have had enough,
> LORD," he said. "Take my life; I am no better than
> my ancestors." Then he lay down under the tree
> and fell asleep.
>
> 1 Kings 19:4–5

If you were to read this biblical passage without knowing anything that preceded it, what do you suppose you would surmise about this man? This man comes to a broom tree (called "juniper tree" in the King James Version), which is a large desert shrub. He sits under it. He prays to die. He tells the Lord he has "had enough." He evaluates himself, and concludes that he is no better than his ancestors. He then falls asleep.

If you knew nothing about the man being described in 1 Kings 19:4–5, you would probably conclude that this person is very tired; indeed, he is exhausted. He has been through some sort of trauma. He believes in God and has some relationship with Him, but he is suicidal; he wants to leave this world. He feels like a total failure. In a word, this person is depressed.

Have you ever been depressed? There are degrees of depression. Almost certainly we all experience a measure of depression at some stage in our lives. It can be temporary or permanent. The latter state is usually called being clinically depressed. This, too, can happen to a genuine Christian. Hymn writer William Cowper almost certainly falls into this category. Elijah, however, was momentarily drained of energy—like having little or no adrenaline at the moment. Sleeping was what he needed. He needed space and time alone.

A Closer Look at Depression

The teaching on depression in this chapter is especially important for us "ordinary humans" because we have many misperceptions about it, and judge ourselves and others unfairly. What are some of these errors?

First, we fail to realize that the best of Christians can sometimes become depressed. It can happen to any of us. The most godly and the most valuable servants of God can lapse into a state of depression. If you have known depression, Elijah's state described above should encourage you—to let you see you are not the first to feel as you do. If you are a Christian and have experienced depression, you may be among those who conclude they must not have been truly converted. That is not true. The great Charles Spurgeon, one of the ablest preachers in Church history, experienced severe bouts of depression in his latter years.

Second, if you happen to be a leader, or a person with some profile, you are especially vulnerable to the kind of satanic attack that Elijah was under. The apostle Paul describes his greatest trial when he "despaired even of life. Indeed, in our hearts we felt the sentence of death" (2 Corinthians 1:8–9). This was, however, as we saw above, to increase his faith "that we might not rely on ourselves but on God, who raises the dead" (verse 9).

Third, we are all capable of extreme depression if we have been overworking and get overtired. We are given one day in seven to rest. Some of us never get that—and we may pay dearly in the end. Even Jesus needed to get away from the crowds. All of us need space and time alone with God. Sometimes God overrules and makes us take a rest. That, in fact, is at the bottom of what was going on in this phase of Elijah's life. God was the architect of the whole scenario.

Fourth, this time in Elijah's life shows that some of the best of God's people have been suicidal. The prophet Jeremiah wished he were dead (see Jeremiah 20:14–18) as did Job (see Job 3:1). Before you criticize a person like this just consider that you have not experienced depression like theirs. Never point the finger at those who have experienced severe depression. Would you be any better?

Realize that depression does not mean possession by the devil. There is a difference between satanic *oppression*—which leaves us depressed—and *possession*—when a person is controlled by the demonic. Elijah was oppressed; Jezebel was possessed.

Fifth, a person under attack, as in severe depression, may not always demonstrate the fruits of the Spirit at a time like that. The fruits of the Spirit are love, joy, peace, patience, kindness, goodness, faithfulness, gentleness and self-control (see Galatians 5:22–23). Some do manage to exude Christ-likeness in a time of depression. We admire them. But these fruits may not always flourish in a time of severe testing.

We all would blush if God showed the world what we are like when we are exhausted and under severe attack of the devil. We are prone to make unguarded comments. We are prone not to turn the other cheek when criticized, but to retort in a carnal manner. Only Jesus, who had the Spirit without limit (see John 3:34), manifested the fruits of the Spirit faithfully, sixty seconds a minute, sixty minutes an hour, 24 hours a day, every day of His life. Be careful that you do not judge a person under severe testing. It could happen to you before this day is over (see Matthew 7:1)!

Sixth, there is more than one cause for depression. There could be a physical cause, such as lack of sleep. Sometimes a chemical imbalance or a glandular malady can cause depression. In the Lord's Prayer, the first petition we ask for ourselves is "Give us today our daily bread" (Matthew 6:11). As I point out in my book *The Lord's Prayer* (Chosen, 2010), this petition refers not only to food but also to essential needs—including sleep. We need to pray for our essential needs even before our spiritual needs are met, the next petition being, "Forgive us our debts, as we also have forgiven our debtors" (Matthew 6:12).

Our Lord, therefore, began with the physical body in this amazing prayer. If we are not well off physically, it is hard to give adequate attention to our spiritual needs. So Elijah was tired. Exhausted. He should not be criticized by you or me for how he felt, what he said about himself or what he prayed for.

There are other causes for depression. There could be emotional or psychological causes that go back to childhood traumas. "As the twig is bent, so is the tree," says Dr. Clyde Narramore, who adds: "Every person is worth understanding." We all have damaged emotions.

That said, depression *can* be rooted in a spiritual problem, such as when a person is not obedient and walking in the light (see 1 John 1:7). God can hide His face to get our attention, especially when we have not persisted in faith as we should or spent time with the Lord as we should. God likes your company; He might allow you to be depressed to drive you to your knees.

God knows exactly what we are going through, and cares about all our feelings. He not only never forgets that we are dust, but shows up never too early, never too late, but always just on time.

The Devil Exploits Our Tiredness

Elijah the tired servant was a targeted man. Satan wanted revenge. The devil had suffered a huge defeat on Mount Carmel. It is the devil's nature to attack the person who has threatened him. From the moment Elijah ordered the killing of all the false prophets, Satan sought to get revenge. Elijah had a target on his back. The devil had a suitable person to use, namely, Jezebel. She vowed to kill Elijah.

You do not have to be a high profile Christian to become a target of the devil. Satan hates all of God's people. The moment you dedicate your heart and life to please the Lord Jesus Christ, the devil takes notice. He will seek to get revenge for your renewal in the things of God. His aim? To discourage you, to demoralize you and to make you want to give up trusting the Lord Jesus.

Elijah was terrified. He was "afraid and ran for his life" (1 Kings 19:3). He had given in to a spirit of fear, which, of course, does not come from God. God has not given us a spirit of fear but rather a "spirit of power, of love and of self-discipline" (2 Timothy 1:7). But in his weakness Elijah caved in. The psalmist said, "[D]o not fret—it leads only to evil" (Psalm 37:8).

There is another aspect to this episode: Elijah was being tested. God does not tempt us (see James 1:13), but He does test us (see Genesis 22:1). Temptation comes from within, when we are drawn away by our own lusts. Testing is part of our being disciplined, being prepared. Testing is what God designs for our growth and opportunity to see how we are maturing. It is encouraging to see growth in ourselves.

"When through fiery trials thy pathway shall lie,
My grace, all-sufficient, shall be thy supply,
The flame shall not hurt thee; I only design
Thy dross to consume, and thy gold to refine."

Anonymous

Thus, Elijah was being tested, but, equally, he was a tired man. He was simply tired. Physically exhausted. And the devil was exploiting this condition. The devil never plays fair. He loves to pounce on a person when he or she is already down. Elijah was an easy target.

Unguarded Comments

Elijah wanted to die. He prayed to die. Have you ever prayed to die? Elijah's wish was never granted; he was later taken to heaven in a whirlwind (see 2 Kings 2:11). When that happened he was surely pleased that God had not answered his prayer to die! We all can make extreme, regrettable statements when we are exhausted and depressed. God knows this. Remember: He knows our frame and considers that we are dust.

Depression can cause to surface things deep in our hearts that we have not uttered previously. This is when an uncontrolled tongue can be a like a spark that lights a forest fire (see James 3:5). When we are tired we are more vulnerable to the unguarded comment. And, yet, if the truth be known, Elijah's comment that "I am no better than my ancestors" was a real Freudian slip! It speaks volumes about Elijah's gigantic ego. Yes, Elijah was a highly motivated, ambitious person. He wanted to excel in every way—in prophetic words, in seeing the miraculous, in standing before kings.

And that is not all. Elijah wanted to be the best who ever was—in virtue, goodness and character. His low estate made him see—to his chagrin—that he was not perfect. His ancestors were not perfect. He had hoped to be the first, but he was "no better" than they were. This devastated him. I would want to say to him, "Whoever said you *were* better, Elijah? Whoever said you *should be*, Elijah?" Elijah had set standards for himself that exceeded what any human being can accomplish. He set personal standards that God Himself does not require. That comment—"I am no better than my ancestors"—tells you an awful lot about this prophetic man. He wanted to be the first. The best. Ever.

To people who have a mega dose of ambition, not to reach their goals is to feel like a failure. To them anything less than unparalleled success is to fail. They lose face in their own eyes. Failure to people like this is to become depressed because they are not the best who ever lived. It is unrealistic, if not silly, but that is what extreme ambition does for people. They need extremely high achievement to feel good about themselves. Elijah wanted to be the best who ever was in faith and moral character.

I am no better than my ancestors.

"Sorry, Elijah," God would seem to be saying. "You have set a standard for yourself that was your own idea; it certainly wasn't Mine!" Elijah wanted to outdo every person who had preceded him—the patriarchs, Moses, Samuel and the best of the kings of Israel. He was a driven man, a quality that usually comes from the way a person is brought up. Sometimes this comes by a father who could never be satisfied with his son or daughter.

Ambition can be a good thing, but, truly, it originates most often in the desire to be admired. According to the writer of Ecclesiastes, "All labor and all achievement spring from man's envy of his neighbor" (Ecclesiastes 4:4); that is, one has the need to make others a bit jealous! But people like this often drive themselves too hard, and when they crash the hurt is great.

But God loved Elijah and provided for him. Elijah needed a time of solitude, to be away from the crowds. He needed safety, which he had in the desert. He needed shelter, which the broom tree provided. And he needed sleep.

14

Touched by an Angel

> All at once an angel touched him and said, "Get up and eat." He looked around, and there by his head was a cake of bread baked over hot coals, and a jar of water. He ate and drank and then lay down again. The angel of the LORD came back a second time and touched him and said, "Get up and eat, for the journey is too much for you." So he got up and ate and drank. Strengthened by that food, he traveled forty days and forty nights until he reached Horeb, the mountain of God. There he went into a cave and spent the night.
>
> 1 Kings 19:5–9

Most of us do not like being awakened by someone when we are in a deep sleep. I myself hate the sound of an alarm clock, but I would gladly make an exception if an angel awakened me!

I might have had something like this happen—once. Many years ago, in 1956, I had an impulse to get up the next morning at five a.m. and pray. I said, "Lord, if this impulse is from You, please wake me up at five a.m." I then forgot about it and went to bed as usual when, lo and behold, I was wide awake in what seemed like the middle of the night. I wondered why. I then remembered that I had asked the Lord to wake me, so I got up and looked at the clock: dead-on five a.m. I saw no angel but I am sure it was the Lord who awakened me. By the way, I asked the Lord to do it again the next day, but I slept right through to seven o'clock. But God did it once, and I can never forget that.

Elijah was not only awakened by an angel; he evidently saw the angel. But there was more: Right before his eyes Elijah saw by his head a cake of bread baked over hot coals and a jar of water. It was near his head so that in his tiredness he did not even have to move much to eat. What a privilege to have an angel care for you and cook your meal! It is impossible to know what Elijah was thinking. He may have been in such a deep sleep that he thought he was dreaming. Or he may have perceived that he was fully awake, but he was so tired he went right back to sleep after eating. Although this was difficult to absorb, he must have known that God was right there with him, and that things were looking very good. He was still a tired, tired man.

The wonderful thing is, although Elijah's most spectacular work was behind him, God was not finished with him. God was right there—tenderly, lovingly and caringly looking after this worn-out prophet. God does not forget us even though our greatest work could be behind us. He loves us as His own children, regardless of our profiles or usefulness to Him.

Now the angel woke Elijah a second time, touched him and spoke: "Get up and eat, for the journey is too much for you." Indeed, considering it took forty days and forty nights to get there. I do not know the significance of the forty days, although it is a time frame that was particularly relevant in Israel's past (see Genesis 7:4; 25:20; 26:34; 50:3; Exodus 16:35; 24:18; Deuteronomy 2:7) and later on in Jesus' day (see Matthew 4:2).

This time Elijah was strengthened by the food and water and headed for Mount Horeb, better known as Mount Sinai, where Moses received the Ten Commandments. Why Horeb or Sinai? We can only guess. I have never personally found that going to a "holy place" brought me closer to God. I have been to nearly all the holy places of Israel several times, but I cannot say I experienced anything except the delight in being there. Some testify otherwise. I have friends who say God has been particularly real to them in certain places in Jerusalem and Galilee. Perhaps Elijah felt good about going where God had done great things in the past. The Lord told Jacob to go back to Bethel, where he had once found God so real (see Genesis 35:1). So God is pleased sometimes to show up at the same place more than once.

Elijah made Mount Carmel famous. He was now going to the mountain Moses made famous. After all, he and Moses would one day be linked together: He and Moses would appear at the Mount of Transfiguration (probably Mount Nebo or Mount Hermon) with Jesus (see Matthew 17:3).

Elijah found a cave at Mount Horeb and spent the night. He must have been exceedingly grateful for this special attention from the angel. But he may also have been so tired that he was not able to absorb this supernatural manifestation of God. In any case, "strengthened by the food," he traveled on forty days and forty nights. With such supernatural manifestations going on you might have thought that the Holy

Spirit alone—without food—would give him strength! But even amidst such power and supernatural manifestations, Elijah still needed food. It is a reminder that as long as we are in these bodies we will need physical sustenance. This shows further why, as we noted earlier, Jesus put physical needs before spiritual in the Lord's Prayer: "Give us this day our daily bread."

About Angels

A brief introduction to angels is in order. Angels—fallen and unfallen—are God's creation (see Colossians 1:16). At some point in time a vast number of them rebelled. They became known as fallen angels. The chief angel, called "Lucifer" (see Isaiah 14:12, KJV) or "morning star"—who became known as Satan—recruited many angels to revolt against God. "I will raise my throne above the stars of God," Satan said (Isaiah 14:13). It is possible that he took one-third of the angels with him (see Revelation 12:4). In any case, God cast them down to hell (Greek, *tartarus*—see 2 Peter 2:4). They, therefore, "did not keep their positions of authority" and are now kept in darkness, awaiting judgment (see Jude 6).

Those angels that did not enter into Satan's revolt against God are called "elect angels" (see 1 Timothy 5:21). They are the ones that minister to us. One of these was chosen to minister to Elijah.

These elect angels are called "ministering spirits sent to serve those who will inherit salvation" (Hebrews 1:14). They are the angels that encamp around those who fear the Lord (see Psalm 34:7). They protect, guide, overrule and sometimes speak to us. They are self-effacing and show utter contempt for our adulation of them, refusing any worship categorically (see Revelation 22:8–9). They worship Jesus Christ (see Hebrews 1:6).

They are apparently able to take on many forms, sometimes appearing as human beings or even as fire (see Exodus 3:2). God can make the supernatural look natural; they may or may not be immediately recognized as angels. They can, for instance, appear as someone baking a cake of bread over coals of fire. They are inflexibly obedient to God; they do as they are told. They may show up anywhere, anytime. We are cautioned not to neglect strangers, since some people of God have entertained angels but were not aware of it (see Hebrews 13:2).

An extraordinary story came out of Norway some years ago. A Norwegian couple—missionaries—were traveling in Canada. They were hungry, out of food and had no money. As they drove into a certain small town, a Chinese man hailed them and they stopped their car. They were urged to come inside to his restaurant, so they accepted the invitation. They explained they had no money. "That is no problem," he assured them.

Inside they admired the immaculately clean restaurant, they were led to a table with a lovely white tablecloth. They were given a beautiful meal and treated kindly. There would be no charge, insisted this Chinese man. After the meal, they went on their way, thanking God for this wonderful moment.

Two years later, when back in that region of Canada, the couple determined to return to that Chinese restaurant to thank the owners for their kindness. They found the same little town and drove to the spot where they had been so graciously welcomed and cared for. But there was no restaurant. They asked around, talking to several people who lived there. "There never has been a Chinese restaurant in this town," they were told.

Have you ever seen an angel? I think I have—once. In the first year or so of my ministry at Westminster Chapel, there was an attendee—an elderly quaint man who always sat alone—whom I had seen two or three times. He came by my vestry one Sunday after the morning service to say something to me. It was a very, very important word for me. It was prophetic and to the point. It was not a word I particularly wanted, but I never forgot it. I never saw him again.

God's Therapy

Elijah could not have known that he was headed for one of the most significant sessions of psychotherapy ever recorded. God is the greatest counselor on the planet. He knows our background backward and forward, knows our plans, ambitions and wishes. Most of all, He knows what is best for us and gives us the way forward; indeed, the next step forward. Elijah was particularly blessed to have God Himself as his analyst and therapist. Would that we all could hear God speak as He did to Elijah! God's therapy combined physical rest, food, gentle probing and counseling, all given to Elijah one step at a time.

Elijah was very fragile. His emotions were almost shut down. He needed space. Plenty of time. Solitude, without voices from all directions telling him what was wrong with him and what he should do. God knew exactly how to handle Elijah.

15

The Elijah Complex

> And the word of the LORD came to him: "What are you doing here, Elijah?"
>
> He replied, "I have been very zealous for the LORD God Almighty. The Israelites have rejected your covenant, broken down your altars, and put your prophets to death with the sword. I am the only one left, and now they are trying to kill me too."
>
> 1 Kings 19:9–10

For three years Elijah had been running from King Ahab, who was looking for him high and low throughout Israel. Now he was running from Jezebel, who had sworn an oath to kill him. She was not able to make good her vow. Running scared to death, Elijah left his servant behind and went deep into the desert. He was tired—very tired—and depressed. An angel showed up, provided food and drink for him, saying only that Elijah should eat. Elijah needed sleep and food. Now here he was at Mount Horeb in a cave, forty days later. He was more rested.

God showed up again and this time asked a question: "What are you doing here, Elijah?" When God asks a question, it is not because He is seeking information (He already knows everything); it was His gentle way to get Elijah to begin talking. God was enabling Elijah to think for himself.

We cannot usually see our faults just because someone has told them to us; we will be defensive and deny them. If we *can* see our faults for ourselves, it is healing. The healing often begins by talking. It is therapeutic to speak when in the presence of a wise, caring friend. The goal in this therapeutic session was to help Elijah come to some objectivity about himself; that is, to see himself as he really was rather than what he thought he was. We have seen how this great prophet had his weaknesses. Now we will see how patiently and gently God dealt with him.

God is that way with all of us. We all have sin, says John (see 1 John 1:8), but God may take years and years before He brings us face-to-face with what we are really like. To see ourselves with total objectivity too soon would destroy us.

Self-Righteousness

What comes out in Elijah's answer shows his self-righteousness: "I have been very zealous for the Lord God Almighty." Self-righteousness is usually the last sin we see in ourselves; it is the hardest to see, the hardest to admit to. For that reason it may take years and years before we begin to see how self-righteous we are. This is a sin most obnoxious to God—and which we find obnoxious in others. God is patient toward us; indeed, far more patient than we are with others.

During the years of our Pilot Light ministry at Westminster Chapel (witnessing in the streets between Victoria and Buckingham Palace), I learned a lot of things, one of them being how self-righteous *all* people are—whether saved or lost, whether atheist or of strong religious background. I discovered, virtually without exception, that everyone—even people who do not believe there is such a thing as God or heaven—*everyone* thinks that if there *is* a heaven, "I will go there because I have been a good person."

Although we must climb down from our self-righteousness to become a Christian—praying, "God, be merciful to me a sinner"—self-righteousness is not eradicated from us by conversion. It lingers on and on. I blush to admit it, but this very year I discovered something about myself that has eluded me all these years. It has to do with my own self-righteousness.

Self-righteousness is basically a feeling of "I'm okay." "I am basically all right." "I am not all that bad or awful." "I am not like other people." "It is not really my fault." "It is your fault." Self-righteousness is the inability to see and then to admit, "I am wrong." We see wrong in others, but almost never in ourselves. We see jealousy and envy in others far more quickly than we see such in ourselves. We see ambitious motives in others before we see them in ourselves. We rarely see ourselves as others do.

> O wad some Power the giftie gie us
> To see oursels as ithers see us!
> Robert Burns (1759–1796)

Self-righteousness is feeling we deserve the credit. Self-pity, the twin of self-righteousness, often comes from feeling we are not getting noticed, not getting the credit.

I have been very zealous for the Lord God Almighty. "You don't seem to notice what I have done for You," Elijah was saying. Elijah was really feeling sorry for himself. Self-pity, like self-righteousness, always seems right and justified at the time. The truth is, it is never justified!

What moves me most is that God does not rebuke him. He does not moralize. He does not slap Elijah's wrist. He just listens. I have referred to Psalm 103:14 several times in this book, and let me do so again: He knows our frame and remembers that we are dust. How gracious and good God is!

So Elijah, having spoken, now proceeds to inform God of a thing or two: "The Israelites have rejected Your covenant, broken down Your altars, and put Your prophets to death by the sword. I am the only one left, and now they are trying to kill me, too." Poor Elijah. It is good to express our feelings, but that we *feel* a certain way does not mean we have got it right. As Alexander Pope said, "All is yellow to the jaundiced eye."

Elijah's self-importance shouts from his self-righteousness. You will recall that this is not the first time Elijah said, "I am the only one left." He said this before everybody on Mount Carmel (see 1 Kings 18:22). God overlooked this false statement then and let Elijah continue. God puts up with so much of what we say that is not true. He does not yank us from the platform or put us out of service or embarrass us before everybody. Time is on His side; He will sort us out down the road.

He did so with Elijah. Later on He said, as it were, "Oh, by the way, Elijah, I reserve seven thousand in Israel—all whose knees have not bowed down to Baal. You are *not* the only one left" (see 1 Kings 19:18). You might have thought that God would sort out Elijah on this important insight *before* his triumph on Mount Carmel. It goes to show that we do not have to be perfected to do our finest work for God. He uses imperfect, frail jars of clay. Best of all, if God can use an Elijah, a man "just like us" (James 5:17), He can use you and me.

Come As You Are

It is precisely this principle that must be grasped concerning hearing and receiving the Gospel. Just as some surmise that you must be totally perfected before you can do your best work for God, so also some teach that you must be sufficiently "prepared" before you can come to Christ.

I faced this issue again and again when I studied the English Puritans at Oxford. There was a feeling among so many Puritans that one cannot come as he or she *is*, but that he or she must be sufficiently prepared before qualifying for saving faith.

This is so wrong. I love the hymns that say,

> Come, ye weary, heavy laden,
> Bruised and broken by the fall;
> If you tarry till you're better,
> You will never come at all:
> Not the righteous . . .
> Sinners Jesus came to call.
>
> Let not conscience make you linger,
> Nor of fitness fondly dream;
> All the fitness he requireth
> Is to feel your need of him;
> This he gives you . . .
> 'Tis the Spirit's rising beam.
> Joseph Hart (1712–1768)

139

Just as I am, without one plea
But that Thy blood was shed for me,
And that Thou bidd'st me come to Thee,
O Lamb of God, I come! I come!
                Charlotte Elliott (1789–1871)

The words of Elijah we are examining in this chapter reveal what many observers have called "the Elijah complex"—the feeling that we are the only ones who are standing for the truth. We see that this feeling is born in self-righteousness and self-pity.

A *complex* is "a connected group of feelings that influence a person's behavior or mental attitude." Sometimes these ideas have been repressed and surface as an exaggerated concern or fear. Some people, for instance, have an inferiority complex, a feeling that they are inferior to others ("I'm not okay, but you're okay"). Some have a superiority complex, a feeling that they are a cut above everybody ("I'm okay, but you're not okay"). Some people have a persecution complex, a feeling that everybody is out to get them. Some have a messianic complex, a feeling that they are destined to be a savior or solver of the world's problems.

The Elijah complex, then, is the feeling of being the only one who has stood for the truth—and who is not getting credit for it. It is, in a sense, a combination of all the complexes described above. Some might say that Elijah said what he did in the cave at Mount Horeb because he was overtired, but the truth is that he had been thinking this all along. It is a danger one faces when one feels one has a mandate from God (which Elijah no doubt had) but is not getting due recognition for it.

As I said, God knew about this weakness in Elijah all along. God might have overlooked this indefinitely, but, for some reason, He decided to break the truth to Elijah gently. It is kind of God to sort us out while we are in this world, before we are glorified (at which time He will finish the job). And there are also times when God reveals the *fuller* truth to us after we have already pontificated on a particular teaching. I know what it is to preach from a text on a Sunday morning, only to find out Monday, when it is too late to explain it publicly, what that text truly meant! So humbling.

The truth is, God was not finished with Elijah yet. What is more, Elijah was shortly to discover one of the most sublime and beautiful ways of God. All of us have more to learn about ourselves—and God.

16

When God Speaks Softly

> The LORD said, "Go out and stand on the mountain in the presence of the LORD, for the LORD is about to pass by." Then a great and powerful wind tore the mountains apart and shattered the rocks before the LORD, but the LORD was not in the wind. After the wind there was an earthquake, but the LORD was not in the earthquake. After the earthquake came a fire, but the LORD was not in the fire. And after the fire came a gentle whisper. When Elijah heard it, he pulled his cloak over his face and went out and stood at the mouth of the cave.
>
> 1 Kings 19:11–13

This passage is arguably the best known from the Elijah story. I refer also to the King James translation and the "still small voice," called here a "gentle whisper."

It would not be wrong to conclude that Elijah was learning his greatest lesson about himself and receiving his greatest insight about God.

This passage shows how God loves to do what is unprecedented. Sometimes He repeats Himself; sometimes He does what He has never done before. This part of the story shows the unpredictable ways of God—how He loves to surprise. It teaches us not to speculate as to what God is going to do next or how He will show up! We all have so much more to learn about God, regardless of how old we are or how long we have been Christians.

Precedents for Wind, Earthquake and Fire

Sometimes God does repeat Himself. Take wind. The first mention of wind in the Bible is in Genesis 8:1, in Noah's day, when God "sent a wind over the earth, and the waters receded." Later on, when Moses stretched out his staff over Egypt, the Lord made "an east wind blow," sending locusts to invade Egypt (Exodus 10:13). The most memorable use of wind is when God sent another east wind and turned the sea into dry land, "with a wall of water" on the right and left, letting the children of Israel cross the Red Sea on dry land (Exodus 14:22). During the time the children of Israel were in the wilderness, "a wind went out from the LORD and drove quail in from the sea" (Numbers 11:31). Elijah himself had had an experience with wind just weeks earlier when he had prayed for rain: The sky grew black with clouds and "the wind rose" (1 Kings 18:45).

Since God had used wind a number of times in the past, Elijah had every reason to suspect that God was now doing it again. "A great and powerful wind tore the mountains apart and shattered the rocks before the Lord." When God repeats Himself it is easier to accept Him. We love the familiar. We all like "old times" to return.

But, lo and behold, "the Lord was not in the wind." How could Elijah tell? I don't know. The wind came immediately after the Lord had commanded Elijah to stand in the mountain in His presence, "for the Lord is about to pass by." Elijah had every reason to believe this was the Lord's manifestation. I would love to know how Elijah knew that God was not in the wind. Perhaps at first he thought He was.

Then came an earthquake. There was also great precedent for this. When Moses was called by the Lord right there on the same mountain hundreds of years before, "Mount Sinai was covered with smoke . . . the whole mountain trembled violently" (Exodus 19:18). It also happened in Samuel's day. As a seal of God upon Jonathan's vision to attack the Philistines, "the ground shook." It was seen as "a panic sent by God" (1 Samuel 14:15). So if God was not in the wind, Elijah may have thought, *This is the Lord*, when the earthquake came. But God was not in the earthquake. How did Elijah know?

The thing is, when something is repeated that was previously clearly the Lord's manifestation, most people assume hastily and uncritically, "This is God showing up again." In fact, some well-meaning people have been known to "work up" something similar to what God did in the past in order to make themselves feel that "glorious days are here again," but it is not the Holy Spirit at all.

Jonathan Edwards taught us that the task of every generation is to discover the direction in which the Sovereign Redeemer is moving, then move in that direction. It is easy to look for what has happened before. There is little stigma in embracing the familiar.

144

"After the earthquake came a fire"—a likely manifestation of the presence of God if there ever was one. First, God sent fire—"burning sulfur"—on Sodom and Gomorrah (Genesis 19:24). A flame of fire appeared in the bush that Moses saw, and which was not consumed (Exodus 3:2–3). The Lord descended on the same Mount Sinai "in fire" (Exodus 19:18). The Lord led the children of Israel through the wilderness with the "pillar of fire" (Exodus 13:22). Moreover, again, Elijah had seen fire fall on Mount Carmel only weeks before. Surely this was God at work. Wrong again! "The Lord was not in the fire."

Elijah was learning more deeply how to discern the true presence of God. He was learning that God is not bound by the way He has shown up in the past. This acute sense of discernment is sorely needed today when people tend to repeat or work up the same old thing as what happened a few years back and call it God. It may not be God at all.

The Unprecedented Manifestation

"After the fire came a gentle whisper" (1 Kings 19:12). "The sound of a low whisper" (ESV). A "still small voice" (KJV). Never before had God shown up like this. Never before had He spoken in this soft, gentle manner. The first time God actually *spoke* (that is recorded) was when He said, "'Let there be light,' and there was light" (Genesis 1:3). The psalmist said,

> The voice of the LORD is powerful; the voice of the LORD is majestic. The voice of the LORD breaks the cedars; the LORD breaks in pieces the cedars of Lebanon . . . shakes the desert . . . twists the oaks and strips the forests bare.
>
> Psalm 29:4–9

Whoever would have predicted that God would speak in a "gentle whisper"? Yet He did.

It was a most profound experience. The writer never explicitly says that the Lord was in the gentle whisper. We only know that "when Elijah heard it, he pulled his cloak over his face and went out and stood at the mouth of the cave." When the seraphim before the throne of God worshiped and called to one another, "Holy, holy, holy is the LORD Almighty; the whole earth is full of his glory," they had wings that "covered their faces" (Isaiah 6:2–3). That is what Elijah did. He pulled his cloak over his face. He knew he was in the immediate presence of God.

I grew up in Kentucky when a preacher had to shout to be trusted! We knew the stories from the Cane Ridge Revival (1802), when, for four days, hundreds were flat-out prostrate on the ground under the power of the Spirit, and came up shouting with great assurance of salvation. They said it was like the "sound of Niagara"—you could hear their voices a mile away.

The preachers of that era raised their voices and often spoke with such vehemence that they gasped between sentences. This to some became a sign of the anointing. Preachers kept it up for a hundred years. You can still hear it today in some Baptist churches in Kentucky—every Sunday. People seem to forget that "a gentle tongue can break a bone" (Proverbs 25:15). Jonathan Edwards' famous sermon in the previous century "Sinners in the Hands of an Angry God" (1741) that shook New England for years was actually read from a manuscript word-for-word in a monotone. It is not the volume but the anointing that makes the difference. And God may choose to do what He has never done before. That is one of the things Elijah was learning.

We had a Prayer Covenant at Westminster Chapel. The members pledged to pray daily for certain petitions we suggested, and among them was this: "We pray for the manifestation of Your glory in our midst along with an ever-increasing openness in us to the way You choose to turn up." I had the Cane Ridge Revival in mind. I was terrified at the thought that God might turn up in conservative Westminster Chapel like that! The petition was aimed to prepare us just in case!

When Elijah stood at the mouth of the cave, he heard the Lord's voice, possibly in the same gentle whisper, asking the same question again: "What are you doing here, Elijah?" Would Elijah's answer be different this time? No. The gentle whisper had not changed his attitude: "I am very zealous for the Lord Almighty. The Israelites have rejected your covenant, broken down your altars, and put your prophets to death with the sword. I am the only one left, and now they are trying to kill me, too."

God's Next Step for Elijah

God still did not rebuke him or correct him. Elijah may have felt more than amply confirmed that he spoke the absolute truth to the Lord. God merely gave Elijah his next set of orders. And at then at the end—as if to say, "Oh, by the way"—He gently reminded Elijah that he was not the only one left after all!

> The LORD said to him, "Go back the way you came, and go to the Desert of Damascus. When you get there, anoint Hazael king over Aram. Also, anoint Jehu son of Nimshi king over Israel, and anoint Elisha son of Shaphat from Abel Meholah to succeed you as prophet. Jehu will put to death any who

escape the sword of Hazael, and Elisha will put to death any
who escape the sword of Jehu. Yet I reserve seven thousand
in Israel—all whose knees have not bowed down to Baal and
all whose mouths have not kissed him."

1 Kings 19:15–18

The Lord made no comment at all regarding Elijah's
claim to be zealous or the fact that he was the "only one
left." It reminds me of Jesus' appearing to the disciples in
the Upper Room after His resurrection. They were feeling
guilty and fearful. They had *so* let the Lord down. Jesus did
not even refer to it; He simply said to them, "Peace be with
you! As the Father has sent me, I am sending you" (John
20:21). In other words, making no mention of what was on
their minds, He simply gave them orders about what was
coming next.

So the Lord said to Elijah, "Go back the way you came,
and go to the Desert of Damascus." How interesting! He
was not to go directly to Damascus but *the way he came*—
which meant going through Jezreel where Jezebel was waiting to kill him. God wanted Elijah to face his fears, overcome them and discover anew that God would protect and
preserve him.

The prophet Elijah needed to exercise faith in a manner
in which he had failed to do a few weeks before. After Jesus'
birth, the Magi were directed to return to the East "by another
route" to avoid King Herod (Matthew 2:12), but Elijah did
not get to go by another route. He had to go back *the way he
came*. He was ordered to do the very thing he feared! If you
start running because you are afraid, where and when do you
stop? It is no victory if fear diminishes because the enemy is
not around; it is a triumph when you have an internal victory

148

over fear with the enemy very much at large. That is what God wanted for Elijah.

Elijah received what might be seen as his final "marching orders." Although less spectacular than calling fire down Mount Carmel, what Elijah now had to do was vital for the immediate future of Israel. He was given three commands: (1) anoint Hazael king of Aram, (2) anoint Jehu to be king over Israel and (3) anoint Elisha to be his own successor.

Then came what was a gentle, subtle—like a tap of a feather on Elijah's shoulder—correction, as if to say, "Oh, by the way, Elijah. I reserve seven thousand in Israel—all whose knees have not bowed down to Baal and all whose mouths have not kissed him."

God took a good while before breaking this bit of news to Elijah. God is in no hurry to correct us. He knows the end from the beginning. He knows us backward and forward when He calls us. For this reason He never gets disillusioned with us; He had no illusions about us in the first place! This is why God can use imperfect people—like you and me.

The Calling of Elisha

I am not sure how thrilled Elijah was at that third command God gave him. It pertained to a successor; he may not have wanted a successor! He may have wanted to be the first and the last of the truly great prophets, the beginning and the end! But he was given detailed information for the immediate future that included who his successor should be.

> So Elijah went from there and found Elisha son of Shaphat. He was plowing with twelve yoke of oxen, and he himself was driving the twelfth pair. Elijah went up to him and threw his cloak around him. Elisha then left his oxen and ran after

Elijah. "Let me kiss my father and mother good-by," he said, "and then I will come with you."

"Go back," Elijah replied. "What have I done to you?"

So Elisha left him and went back. He took his yoke of oxen and slaughtered them. He burned the plowing equipment to cook the meat and gave it to the people, and they ate. Then he set out to follow Elijah and became his attendant.

1 Kings 19:19–21

God had chosen Elijah's successor; it was out of his hands. Elijah had nothing to say about it. This is a reminder that it is God's Kingdom, not ours, of which we are a small part! The anointing of a prophet is as important as the anointing of a king. The things pertaining to God's spiritual Kingdom—the Church—are as important as the things that pertain to His visible Kingdom—the state.

God does not always raise up successors. Joshua had no successor. Samuel had no successor. Elisha would have no successor. Why? You tell me. Some eras end; some continue. Some eras you want to end. If God is doing something wonderful you want it to continue.

Elijah had to go 160 miles to find Elisha. No inconvenience is too great to find the right person. It does not matter where a person is from, or what his prestigious qualifications might be. What matters is what God wants.

Elisha was found plowing. Who would have thought that this man would be the successor to the great Elijah! But as the Lord said on another occasion, "Do not consider his appearance or his height. . . . The LORD does not look at the things man looks at. Man looks at the outward appearance, but the LORD looks at the heart" (1 Samuel 16:7). God saw gifts in Elisha that might not have been apparent to anybody else. God was looking for a man who would be willing to be a servant of a prophet rather than the master of a large farm.

In any case, it was a sudden shift in Elisha's life. He was not prepared for this, but he went along. He "set out to follow Elijah and became his attendant."

17

Evil, Justice and Mercy

> There was never a man like Ahab, who sold him-
> self to do evil in the eyes of the LORD, urged on by
> Jezebel his wife. He behaved in the vilest manner
> by going after idols.
>
> 1 Kings 21:25–26

God was not finished with Elijah. He would be suddenly summoned by the Holy Spirit to speak once
more into the lives of King Ahab and Queen Jezebel.
God had said to His people long before this: "It is mine
to avenge; I will repay. In due time their foot will slip" (Deuteronomy 32:35). Elijah was not getting personal vengeance
with the words he proclaimed to the royal couple. He carried
no grudge against Jezebel for her vow to kill him. As far as I
know, he had no idea of being brought again into the lives of
Ahab and Jezebel, but events transpired that required Elijah's

intervention for something else they were involved in. God determined to step in and judge wickedness in the palace.

Ahab coveted a vineyard that was located nearby. It belonged to Naboth of Jezreel. The king wanted to buy it or trade for it, as it was a convenient spot for a vegetable garden. The vineyard, however, was Naboth's family inheritance, and he did not want to give it up. This caused Ahab to sulk.

Jezebel noticed his sullen spirit and asked why. He told his wife he was upset because he could not get Naboth's vineyard. She chided him, "Is this how you act as king over Israel? Get up and eat! Cheer up. I'll get you the vineyard." She set the innocent Naboth up as a person who had cursed God and the king, whereupon Naboth was taken outside the city and stoned to death. She then reported Naboth's death to Ahab who unashamedly took possession of the vineyard.

Enter Elijah. His prophetic gift was needed. He was not tapped to speak into the situation because of Jezebel's previous vow to kill him. There was, I repeat, nothing personal in Elijah's reentering King Ahab's life. God was judging Ahab's wife not for vowing to kill Elijah but for masterminding Naboth's cruel and unjust death. When a person as evil as Jezebel is around, it is only a matter of time until wickedness is compounded and, finally, God steps in.

This account is relevant for someone who has experienced gross injustice. If you have experienced evil done to you by someone, wait. Sit back. Do nothing. This person will continue to do evil elsewhere. You might feel a little peeved that he or she is judged for what he or she does to someone *else*— and not you! But never mind. Let God be God. Be careful never—ever—to take vengeance into your own hands. It is God's business to do this. And He does it so brilliantly that you would be foolish to help Him out in the slightest manner.

God is slow to anger, but when He does step in He shows how He is fully aware of all the evil that has taken place, and carries out justice clearly, decisively and awesomely.

> Then the word of the LORD came to Elijah the Tishbite: "Go down to meet Ahab king of Israel, who rules in Samaria. He is now in Naboth's vineyard, where he has gone to take possession of it. Say to him, 'This is what the LORD says: Have you not murdered a man and seized his property?' Then say to him, 'This is what the LORD says: In the place where dogs licked up Naboth's blood, dogs will lick up your blood—yes, yours!'"
>
> 1 Kings 21:17–19

What a privilege to have a relationship with God that is so intimate that God can speak to you verbatim about a situation! God knows people's names, where they live and what they have done. When God shares His heart with us, we are honored. Elijah was off the hook insofar as having to come up with the right words whereby to confront Ahab. God told him what to say, word for word.

But there was more. Elijah was told not only to reveal God's anger and judgment regarding what Jezebel and Ahab had done, but also to prophesy his horrible death: "Dogs will lick up your blood." To say something like this one has to be *sure*. Elijah, operating at an oath level of communication, was sure.

Ahab now gave a new name to Elijah: "Ahab said to Elijah, 'So you have found me, my enemy!'" (1 Kings 21:20). You will recall that Ahab previously referred to Elijah as "troubler of Israel." Here he is called Ahab's enemy. So sad! Ahab had seen the fire of God fall on Mount Carmel; he had witnessed it firsthand. You would think this would surely turn him around. Strange. But he was blinded by Satan.

What is equally interesting is that Ahab was surprised that Elijah knew where he was. "*You have found me*, my enemy!" This demonstrates that we cannot run from God successfully if God wants to find us. God knows our names, addresses, what we did yesterday, where we are today—and every detail of our thoughts. "Nothing in all creation is hidden from God's sight. Everything is uncovered and laid bare before the eyes of him to whom we must give account" (Hebrews 4:13).

Elijah would not have known where Ahab was had Elijah not been specifically told. True prophets are not clairvoyants. They are ordinary people to whom God chooses to reveal things. I fear that there are those around who claim to be prophets but who have a gift that is either of the flesh or the devil and not bathed in the blood of Christ or immersed in the Holy Spirit. They might even deceive the very elect, if possible (see Matthew 24:24).

> "I have found you," [Elijah] answered, "because you have sold yourself to do evil in the eyes of the LORD. 'I am going to bring disaster on you. I will consume your descendants and cut off from Ahab every last male in Israel—slave or free. I will make your house like that of Jeroboam son of Nebat and that of Baasha son of Ahijah, because you have provoked me to anger and have caused Israel to sin.' And also concerning Jezebel the LORD says: 'Dogs will devour Jezebel by the wall of Jezreel.' Dogs will eat those belonging to Ahab who die in the city, and the birds of the air will feed on those who die in the country."
>
> 1 Kings 21:20–24

In this solemn prophecy Elijah has forecast a violent death for Jezebel—she would be devoured by dogs—as we saw, similarly for Ahab—dogs would lick up his blood.

The Jezebel Spirit

Jezebel herself was not the last to have evil influence over the people of God. Many pastors of churches over the years have had to combat what is known as a "Jezebel spirit."

It is deadly: When it gets into a church the smell of death pervades; the church will not be able to grow.

It is destructive: It can bring a church to ruin.

It is divisive: It splits friends and families in churches.

It is demonic: Its origin is from Satan himself.

It is demoralizing to church leaders: It has put many good pastors out of the ministry.

One could write a book on this alone; indeed, some good books have been written on this. To summarize, here are hallmarks of the spirit of Jezebel.

It is a *critical* spirit. There is nothing positive about the influence of Jezebel. It is always critical of what God wants to do, as when Jezebel vowed to kill Elijah for ridding Israel of the false prophets. Where there is a Jezebel, there is constant faultfinding, whether with the leadership or with good people who want to see the honor of God.

It is a *conniving* spirit. It works behind the scenes to cause evil, as when Jezebel had "two scoundrels to testify that Naboth has cursed both God and the king. Then take him out and stone him to death." Jezebel connived to get Naboth out of the way just so Ahab could take over the vineyard he wanted. The people being used generally do not know that Jezebel has orchestrated the evil.

It is a *controlling* spirit. Instead of setting others free, it is a spirit that dominates, takes charge and abides no contrary opinion. Jesus chose to refer to a particular person in the church of Thyatira as "Jezebel," who led Christ's servants into "sexual immorality and the eating of food sacrificed to idols" (Revelation 2:20). Ahab himself was evil, but he was also "urged on by" his wife. Woe to the man who is married to a Jezebel!

It is a *competitive* spirit. It is the opposite of self-effacing. It wants to be "top dog" and regarded as holding to the most important opinion. Whether in a marriage or a church, where there is a Jezebel, there is always a spirit of competition in the air. Jezebel cannot bear the thought of not getting her way. In a marriage where there is a Jezebel, nearly everything between the husband and wife is a contest.

It is a *contagious* spirit. It will spread through the Body of Christ like a cancer. It must be cut out immediately or Satan will succeed in completely destroying a church.

Fortunately, there was an Elijah around who could step in as he did. There is a God in heaven who avenges. When you are confronted with a Jezebel you must pray on bended knee that God will step in. Pray for wisdom, pray for God to overrule. It just may be that God has allowed a Jezebel to thrive for a while to bring His people to their knees. I have seen God turn things around in my own ministry. He will do it for you.

Mercy toward Ahab

Now, something quite extraordinary is to be seen. God, amazingly, showed mercy upon Ahab. Although there had been no king as evil as Ahab, the Lord said to Elijah: "Have you noticed how Ahab has humbled himself before me?" (1 Kings 21: 29). After Elijah had delivered this stunning word to Ahab that prophesied the deaths of Jezebel and himself, Ahab had "[torn] his clothes, put on sackcloth and fasted. He lay in sackcloth and went around meekly" (verse 27).

I do not think anyone expected this, not even Elijah. The question I ask is: Why did Ahab not humble himself at Mount Carmel? Why did he humble himself only after he heard Elijah's somber prophecy? I have no idea. But it does show that, despite all we have seen in Ahab, there must have been a spark of life in him. Who would ever have thought that he would wear sackcloth and fast?

This behavior, however, would not change the prophecy: Elijah had spoken the oath of God. When God speaks at the level of oath, nothing will change what was said. Indeed, later on, after the king died, "the dogs licked up his blood, as the word of the LORD had declared" (1 Kings 22:38). But Ahab's fasting did have this result: God postponed the disaster of cutting off all of Ahab's male descendants until later on, "in the days of [Ahab's] son" (1 Kings 21:29).

I do not understand all this, but it tells me one thing: God is rich in mercy. If you feel you have sinned to the extreme, that there is no hope for you because of the evil you have done, remember wicked Ahab who at the last minute tried to get God's attention. God noticed when Ahab humbled himself. God is amazing. It is a pretty strong hint (if you ask me) that *anybody*—as long as he or she is alive—can ask God for mercy and be given it.

As for Jezebel, no sign of repentance was shown in her. Thus, some time later, "when they went out to bury her, they found nothing except her skull, her feet and her hands." When her death was reported to King Jehu, he said: "This is the word of the LORD that he spoke through his servant Elijah the Tishbite: On the plot of ground at Jezreel dogs will devour Jezebel's flesh" (2 Kings 9:35–36).

18

A Prophet's Vindication

After Ahab's death . . . Ahaziah [king of Israel] had fallen through the lattice of his upper room in Samaria and injured himself. So he sent messengers, saying to them, "Go and consult Baal-Zebub, the god of Ekron, to see if I will recover from this injury."

But the angel of the LORD said to Elijah the Tishbite, "Go up and meet the messengers of the king of Samaria and ask them, 'Is it because there is no God in Israel that you are going off to consult Baal-Zebub, the god of Ekron?' Therefore this is what the LORD says: 'You will not leave the bed you are lying on. You will certainly die!'" So Elijah went.

When the messengers returned to the king, he asked them, "Why have you come back?"

"A man came to meet us," they replied. "And he said to us, 'Go back to the king who sent you and tell him, "This is what the LORD says: Is it

> because there is no God in Israel that you are sending men to consult Baal-Zebub, the god of Ekron? Therefore you will not leave the bed you are lying on. You will certainly die!"'"
>
> The king asked them, "What kind of man was it who came to meet you and told you this?"
>
> They replied, "He was a man with a garment of hair and with a leather belt around his waist."
>
> The king said, "That was Elijah the Tishbite."
>
> 2 Kings 1:1–8

This is the first time we learn a little bit about Elijah's outward appearance. His reputation had begun to precede him: The new king Ahaziah knew instantly who was behind the prophetic word that forecast his own death. He knew this once he heard that it was a man "with a garment of hair and with a leather belt around his waist." It was "Elisha the Tishbite."

Ahaziah no doubt had heard all about Elijah from his parents, Ahab and Jezebel. Hundreds of years later when John the Baptist, who went before the Lord "in the spirit and power of Elijah" (Luke 1:17), preached in the desert of Judea, his "clothes were made of camel's hair, and he had a leather belt around his waist" (Matthew 3:4).

It is immediately obvious that the worship of Baal had returned. The triumph at Mount Carmel did not last. Evil will always return in this world—until Jesus comes a second time. The devil and all evil will be judged and put away forever (see Revelation 20:10). King Ahaziah had had an accident and wanted to know if he would recover. As people today consult a witch or an astrology chart, so Ahaziah consulted Baal-Zebub.

But God was still on Israel's case: An angel of the Lord spoke to Elijah to intervene and ask why the king had not consulted the God of Israel. Then Elijah added his own prophecy: The king would not leave the bed he was lying on, but would die. I am sure that when Ahaziah heard that this word came from Elijah it shocked him rigid from head to toe. The king sent for Elijah.

> Then he sent to Elijah a captain with his company of fifty men. The captain went up to Elijah, who was sitting on the top of a hill, and said to him, "Man of God, the king says, 'Come down!'"
>
> Elijah answered the captain, "If I am a man of God, may fire come down from heaven and consume you and your fifty men!" Then fire fell from heaven and consumed the captain and his men.
>
> At this the king sent to Elijah another captain with his fifty men. The captain said to him, "Man of God, this is what the king says, 'Come down at once!'"
>
> "If I am a man of God," Elijah replied, "may fire come down from heaven and consume you and your fifty men!" Then the fire of God fell from heaven and consumed him and his fifty men.
>
> So the king sent a third captain with his fifty men. This third captain went up and fell on his knees before Elijah. "Man of God," he begged, "please have respect for my life and the lives of these fifty men, your servants! See, fire has fallen from heaven and consumed the first two captains and all their men. But now have respect for my life!"
>
> The angel of the LORD said to Elijah, "Go down with him; do not be afraid of him." So Elijah got up and went down with him to the king.
>
> 2 Kings 1:9–15

Instant vindication is not promised in the Scriptures. As we saw above, vengeance belongs to God, and it is His prerogative—and His alone—to send vengeance or to vindicate. To vindicate means to have your name cleared.

It is a word that became very important to me more than fifty years ago when my decisions caused my own dad to question my direction. I had embraced a theology different from what I had been taught in my old denomination and it deeply upset my father.

His disapproval hurt more than anything I had suffered up to then—namely, to have my own father question my devotion to God or my sense of being led by the Holy Spirit. I longed, therefore, for vindication more than anything I had ever wanted. I actually had to wait 22 years for it, when, on a train coming from Edinburgh to London's King Cross, my dad looked at me and said, "Son, I am proud of you; you were right and I was wrong." Twenty-two years is a long time to wait.

Elijah was more fortunate this time. He got vindication virtually on the spot! He wanted the new King Ahaziah to be ashamed for turning to Baal-Zebub and not to the God of Israel. Sadly, Ahaziah was no better than his parents, Ahab and Jezebel. Elijah also feared that Ahaziah might harm him if he answered the king's order to approach him immediately. This is why two lots of fifty men were destroyed by fire falling from heaven. The king should have known from this that Elijah represented the true God, the God of Israel, and should be feared. The fire falling twice—it was almost like Mount Carmel all over again—was instant vindication for Elijah.

The third group got the message in time, and saved their lives. The third captain—"on his knees before Elijah"—pleaded for his life and the lives of the fifty men. The angel then told Elijah, "Go down with him, and do not be afraid of him." So Elijah went.

A Word to Prophetic People

Moses, long before, had set a standard for prophets: "If what a prophet proclaims in the name of the LORD does not take place or come true, that is a message the LORD has not spoken. That prophet has spoken presumptuously. *Do not be afraid of him*" (Deuteronomy 18:22, emphasis added).

We do not need to fear if we speak against someone whose track record is riddled with misstatements and whose prophecies do not come true. A true prophet is one whose words do not "fall to the ground" (1 Samuel 3:19), an expression meaning that their prophecies do not come to nothing but are absolutely true. That then is the sign of a true prophet. Such men and women are exceedingly rare.

This should be sufficient and sober warning to any person who thinks he or she might have a prophetic gift. This person should be very humble, be careful when making claims of prophetic implications and—above all—be most hesitant to bring in the name of the Lord when offering a prophetic word. It is a scary thing to do. It is the biggest mistake prophetic people make. They do it all the time, and miss it all the time—but then they keep on doing the same thing. It is so wrong. It grieves the Holy Spirit. This person is better off to keep God's name out of his or her prophecies. If they come true, all will see they were indeed words from the Lord; if not, how disgraceful if the prophet claimed, "The Lord told me"!

This is one of the reasons Jesus said we should not swear at all (see Matthew 5:34)—that is, claim to have an authentic word while using the name of the Lord to legitimize it. It is a violation of the Third Commandment: Do not "misuse the name of the LORD your God" (Exodus 20:7). People think erroneously that the Third Commandment refers merely to cursing or swearing. Hardly. It refers mainly to bringing the name of the Lord into our conversations to authenticate ourselves. It is misusing God's name—not only not making Him look good, but also trying to make ourselves look good. Prophetic people should learn to get their vindication by the Spirit, as Jesus did (see 1 Timothy 3:16)—that is, know that God approves without trying to get others to see it.

Elijah now approached the king and delivered the word that the king had heard earlier from his messengers. Here it comes from the lips of Elijah himself: "This is what the Lord says: Is it because there is no God in Israel for you to consult that you have sent messengers to consult Baal-Zebub, the god of Ekron? Because you have done this, you will never leave the bed you are lying on. You will certainly die!" What a word to be told just before you die! Who knows what good thing might have taken place had Ahaziah humbled himself as his father, Ahab, did? "So he died, according to the word of the Lord that Elijah had spoken."

Elijah had a double vindication: first, by the fire falling on the two lots of fifty men; second, by King Ahaziah dying as was prophesied. Vindication is something God delights to give, in His own time. Sometimes it comes soon. Usually, however, it means waiting, and sometimes waiting for a long time. In the meantime, we should lower our voices, not claim too much and let God clear our names.

If our names are not cleared, that is not the worst thing in the world! Far better to have the truth come out in the Final Day that we are genuine, than for people today to think that we are real and find out at the Judgment Seat of Christ that we are false!

Personally I would prefer vindication by the Spirit a million times over—when I feel the pleasure of God on me—than the hollow praise of people. Indeed, I would rather receive God's "Well done" at the Judgment than the acclaim of people today, which is not worth anything at all.

19

Do You Really Want More of God?

When the LORD was about to take Elijah up to heaven in a whirlwind, Elijah and Elisha were on their way from Gilgal. Elijah said to Elisha, "Stay here; the LORD has sent me to Bethel."

But Elisha said, "As surely as the LORD lives and as you live, I will not leave you." So they went down to Bethel.

The company of the prophets at Bethel came out to Elisha and asked, "Do you know that the LORD is going to take your master from you today?"

"Yes, I know," Elisha replied, "but do not speak of it."

Then Elijah said to him, "Stay here, Elisha; the LORD has sent me to Jericho."

And he replied, "As surely as the LORD lives and as you live, I will not leave you." So they went to Jericho.

The company of the prophets at Jericho went up to Elisha and asked him, "Do you know that

> the LORD is going to take your master from you today?"
>
> "Yes, I know," he replied, "but do not speak of it."
>
> Then Elijah said to him, "Stay here; the LORD has sent me to the Jordan."
>
> And he replied, "As surely as the LORD lives and as you live, I will not leave you." So the two of them walked on.
>
> 2 Kings 2:1–6

Charles Spurgeon once said that if a text gets ahold of you, chances are you have got ahold of it. If that is true, I have truly got ahold of this passage above! I do not think I can describe what it means to me. I will say only that it has gripped me over the years like no other passage when it comes to praying for a greater anointing of the Holy Spirit (which I want more than anything).

Two of my Old Testament heroes are Caleb and Elisha. When it was time to enter into Canaan—the Promised Land—God sent twelve spies (one from each of the twelve tribes) to investigate. When the twelve spies returned, ten of them brought a negative report. "The people who live there are powerful, too great to be conquered," they said.

But Caleb silenced the people. With Joshua's support he said, "We should go up and take possession of the land, for we can certainly do it."

"No," said the other ten spies. "These people are of great size. We seemed like grasshoppers in our own eyes, and we looked the same to them" (see Numbers 13:30–33).

167

Sadly the majority ruled; the people chose not to go in. God swore in His wrath that they, therefore, most certainly would *not* enter in (see Hebrews 3:11). They changed their minds, tried the next day and failed miserably, for an oath is irrevocable. In any case, Caleb was one who said in so many words, "Let's go for it," but he was outvoted.

My other hero is Elisha, God's chosen successor to Elijah. We do not know why God chose Elisha. Surely there must have been someone qualified to succeed Elijah closer to where Elijah lived. But no, Elijah traveled 160 miles—into Syria—to find the successor God wanted.

I do not know what quality was in Elisha that made God choose him, but I think it was this: Elisha wanted to get all he could from Elijah before Elijah was taken away. He may not have seen much of Elijah over the years or have been tutored adequately by him (Elisha may have felt particularly ungifted), but he knew one thing: Elijah had something he wanted. Today we call it *anointing*. He was not going to take no for an answer!

In a word: Elisha was not going to let Elijah out of his sight. He did not risk even turning his head away from Elijah. He wanted all he could possibly get from him more than anything he wanted in his life, and he was not going to take any chance that Elijah would slip away while he was looking in another direction. Talk about being focused!

This is how you and I must seek God. We must be focused, adamant, persistent, not looking to the right or left, gazing straight at our Lord and not giving up—like Jacob wrestling with the angel. Jacob said to him, "I will not let you go unless you bless me" (Genesis 32:26). That, in my opinion, is what God saw in Elisha that He did not see in others in Israel. He was not looking for a high IQ, education, culture or a man with a trained mind. He chose a man who had the capacity to want more of God than he wanted anything in the world.

Some people say they want more of God, but the urge or yearning soon wears off. People will come forward in a church service when the sermon is strong. They hear an inspiring anthem. Whatever. But the hunger dissipates with so many who start out strong and eager. They give up.

A. W. Tozer used to say that you can have as much of God as you want. When I first heard that I said, "Not true, I don't have all of God that I want," but I later became convinced he was right. The "want" will be satisfied *if we keep wanting and keep seeking.* What happens, for example, when obstacles are put in your way, whether from God or Satan? What happens when the Lord begins to chasten or discipline you? How soon we give up if there is not the smell of roses, the taste of strawberries and cream or the quick answer to prayer!

Brylcreem Religion

An old friend of mine—Ed Ketner, who is now in heaven—used to preach a sermon called "Brylcreem Religion," the idea being "a little dab'll do ya!" based upon the 1950s television commercial of a hair ointment called Brylcreem. With most people "a little dab" of the Lord is all they want. It reminds me of another friend of mine—Rolfe Barnard, also now in heaven—who was told this by a host pastor where Rolfe was preaching: "We all want revival. We all pray for the Lord's blessing. *But we don't want a stir.*" By that he meant: We don't want to get people upset.

Too many are content with folk religion. Enough to give them a pious feeling on Sunday mornings. Enough to give them a good feeling they will go to heaven when they die.

But it is not a day and night seven-day-a-week passion. With my own nation in the shape it is now in (as I write in 2012), something needs to stir us if we are going to survive at all!

Learning God's Ways

Elisha's persistence in hanging close to Elijah is an illustration of one of God's ways: God wants to be chased. He wants you to seek Him. He often plays "hard to get." Like it or not, this is one of His ways. Moses said to God, "If you are pleased with me, *teach me your ways*" (Exodus 33:13, emphasis added). That is what Moses wanted more than anything.

God grieved over ancient Israel because "they have not known my ways" (Hebrews 3:10). Now He wants to know if *you* care about His ways. You may not like His ways, but He is the only God you have! "'For my thoughts are not your thoughts, neither are your ways my ways,' declares the Lord" (Isaiah 55:8). You must decide whether you want to know the God of the Bible or not. And one of God's ways is that He wants to be chased.

I call it the Divine Tease. God teases us playfully to see if we want Him so much that we will go right against what we thought He was telling us! When Jesus appeared to the two men on the road to Emmaus, He acted as if He was going to go farther, but they urged Him to stay with them—which is what He wanted them to do (see Luke 24:28–29). God said to Moses, "Leave me alone so that my anger may burn against them [the wayward children of Israel] and that I may destroy them. Then I will make you into a great nation" (Exodus 32:9–10). Moses protested: No! "Why should your anger burn against your people, whom you brought out of Egypt with great power and a mighty hand?" (verse 11). Moses pointed out that God's great name was at stake. "Then the LORD relented and did not bring on his people the disaster he had threatened" (verse 14). This was exactly what God wanted Moses to do. Moses was getting to know God's ways. He wants to be pursued and pleaded with.

So we see that Elisha displayed certain knowledge of God's ways when he would not let Elijah out of his sight. Question: Do you have a desire to seek God like that? How much of the anointing of the Holy Spirit do you really want?

Another one of God's ways is His unpredictable manner of choosing sovereign vessels. This phrase is often used to describe special people for service—those like Elijah or Elisha who have been raised up for higher profile ministries. There was, for example, a "company of the prophets" around during this time. One would have thought that God would surely select one or more of them to succeed Elijah. You will recall that Obadiah had protected a hundred prophets from Ahab. What were they hoping to do one day?

There were many young men studying for ministry in England in the nineteenth century, but virtually none of them is known today—only Charles Spurgeon who had no university degree or was even ordained. Spurgeon, in fact, refused ordination. "Their empty hands on my empty head will not add to my empty ministry," he said. He was the greatest preacher of his century; his sermons are still in print today! In much the same way that other ministers were passed over and Spurgeon was chosen, so God passed over the "prophets" and found a man plowing corn—Elisha. "Who has known the mind of the Lord? Or who has been his counselor?" (Romans 11:34).

It is to the credit of these prophets that they acknowledged Elisha as the man to succeed Elijah. Graciousness is a greater virtue than prophetic gifting. I have thought that Caleb might have been the one to succeed Moses, but it was Joshua. There is no hint of a rival spirit between Joshua and Caleb. God is looking for men and women who will affirm the sovereign will of the Spirit, even if we may be disappointed in His choices.

Everybody Knew That Elijah Was Leaving

For some unknown reason, everybody at the time seemed to know that Elijah was going to be transported to heaven. There is no specific word on this, only the consensus from the company of the prophets to Elisha: "Do you know that the Lord is going to take your master from you today?" It must have been revealed to them, but also to Elisha who said: "Yes, I know, but do not speak of it." This certainly led to some mixed feelings; I doubt anybody was happy about Elijah being removed from them. In any case, a great feeling of awe must have pervaded everyone's thoughts on this historic day.

What we have seen above as the Divine Tease, or God playing "hard to get," is now mirrored in Elijah. On their way to Gilgal, knowing that he would be taken shortly, he said to Elisha: "Stay here; the Lord has sent me to Bethel."

Not a chance, said Elisha. "As surely as the Lord lives and as you live, I will not leave you." This was oath language: Elisha put himself under oath—"As surely as the Lord lives," bringing in the Lord, and "as surely as you live," swearing even by Elijah himself. It was Elisha's clear vow not to leave Elijah's side. Nothing could be clearer; there was no way that Elisha would slip away from Elijah.

This rugged intention not to leave Elijah's presence is exactly the way we must be in our plea for God to bless us. Elijah was testing Elisha: "Stay here, I'm going to Bethel." It was, as we noted earlier, like Jesus on the road to Emmaus, when

He acted as if He were going farther, or the Lord walking on water, as if He would pass by, or God telling Moses He would destroy the Israelites and start all over again with him.

The truth is, Jesus wanted the two men to beg for him to stay; He wanted the disciples to cry out to Him on the water; God wanted Moses to intercede for His people. It is the Divine Tease, God's way of testing us to see what is really in our hearts. So, too, with Elijah telling Elisha to stay put while he left for Bethel. Elisha began passing the test. They went together down to Bethel.

There was more. Elijah said to Elisha, "Stay here; the Lord has sent me to Jericho." Elisha might have said to himself, *I showed Elijah I would stay with him and went to Bethel with him. I don't need to keep doing this.* But, no, Elisha was not budging. "As surely as the Lord lives and as you live, I will not leave you." So they went together to Jericho.

Taking Risks

When I took some risks at Westminster Chapel—such as inviting Arthur Blessitt to preach to us during the month of May in 1982—I proved (in the face of criticism) that I was willing to do something new and different. At another time, we began our Pilot Light ministry: We sang choruses in the Chapel, and I gave invitations for people to come forward after the Sunday night services. I nearly got thrown out! The crisis lasted close to four years. It was a horrible time. I said, "Never again"—that is, never again would I take any risk like that. I had proved I would do it; I decided that once was enough!

That is, until I was met with yet another challenge: to welcome prophetic ministry into the Chapel. I thought, *Here we go again*. Not only that, in the 1990s I welcomed into Westminster Chapel what was then called the "Toronto Blessing." I still get emails from people who cannot believe I would do something like that. Nasty comments about me have been put on the Internet, too. All of this was a test to see how much I wanted the blessing of the Holy Spirit.

As I look back on our 25 years at Westminster Chapel, I have to say that true revival never came. We had some moments when the Holy Spirit came in a real and definite way. We had a number of genuine healings and a good number of people truly converted, but what I longed for did not come. Even so, I can look back on those years and know that I did everything I knew to do to please God. I have no regrets.

I am convinced of one thing: Had I been focused on filling the spacious Westminster Chapel from top to bottom, I would not have been open to Arthur Blessitt or prophetic people like John Arnott and Rodney Howard-Browne. I learned so much, and my anointing has increased without a doubt; still, it simply did not result in what I hoped for.

The company of the prophets kept telling Elisha, "Do you know that the Lord is going to take your master from you today?" He had already told them once that he knew; why did they keep this up? It was painful for Elisha to hear. He acknowledged that he knew very well indeed that Elijah's departure was at hand, but he was in no mood to talk about it.

Elijah continued to test his successor—yet again: "Stay here; the Lord has sent me to the Jordan." Elisha repeated his vow: "As surely as the Lord lives and as you live, I will not leave you," so the two of them walked together. Elisha was proving that he would not let Elijah out of his sight. He showed he wanted something from Elijah more than he wanted anything in the world.

What price are you willing to pay for more of God? For a greater anointing? How far are you willing to go in your commitment to Jesus Christ? The latter question was put to me more than once by Josif Tson—the man whose word to me, "You must totally forgive them—or you will be in chains"—changed my life forever. He also kept asking, "How far are you willing to go?" That question was never far from my mind when I had to make hard decisions. I would have far preferred for the Lord to use me alone—directly and without any help from outside guests—but I had to accept that I needed input from others.

Elisha knew he must take advantage of every available moment with Elijah. There was not much time left. He had no way of knowing what the result would be, whether or not, for instance, Elijah would lay hands on him. Nothing would deter Elisha. He was committed.

Commitment is a conscious irrevocable decision. It means you know what you are doing; there will be no turning back from this act of the will. Some people get a religious feeling and make a public commitment—and never show up again. God is not looking for a "flash in the pan" promise from you. He wants to know: How far are you willing to go in your commitment to Jesus Christ?

20

Welcome Home, Elijah

Fifty men of the company of the prophets went and stood at a distance, facing the place where Elijah and Elisha had stopped at the Jordan. Elijah took his cloak, rolled it up and struck the water with it. The water divided to the right and to the left, and the two of them crossed over on dry ground.

When they had crossed, Elijah said to Elisha, "Tell me, what can I do for you before I am taken from you?"

"Let me inherit a double portion of your spirit," Elisha replied.

"You have asked a difficult thing," Elijah said, "yet if you see me when I am taken from you, it will be yours—otherwise not."

As they were walking along and talking together, suddenly a chariot of fire and horses of fire appeared and separated the two of them, and Elijah went up to heaven in a whirlwind. Elisha

> saw this and cried out, "My father! My father!
> The chariots and horsemen of Israel!" And Elisha
> saw him no more. Then he took hold of his own
> clothes and tore them apart.
>
> He picked up the cloak that had fallen from
> Elijah and went back and stood on the bank of
> the Jordan.
>
> 2 Kings 2:7–13

Southern Baptist missionary Henry Morrison and his wife were on a ship coming home after forty years of service in Africa. As the ship neared the New York Harbor the cheering crowds were out, a band was playing.

"They didn't forget us after all," he said to his wife.

As they prepared to disembark a policeman said to him, "Stop here, sir," whereupon the couple stood back and waited. It turned out that President Theodore Roosevelt was on the same ship. The president was coming home after three weeks of big game hunting in Africa.

When the old missionaries finally got to the bottom of the gangplank, they set their suitcases down and looked around. The crowds and the band were flocking around the president; nobody was there to meet them. They made their way to an old hotel a few blocks away. The old missionary, feeling sorry for himself and feeling a little bitter, fell on his knees. "Lord," he said, "I come home and nobody is here to meet me—after forty years of working for you in Africa. President Roosevelt comes home after three weeks game hunting in Africa and the bands play for him."

He then felt the Lord's hand on his shoulder, saying to him, *But you're not home yet.*

I love happy deathbed stories of people seeing a glimpse of heaven or even of Jesus just before they die. I know several stories, some about people I have known. John Wesley used to say to his critics, "Our people die well." My favorite Puritan is John Cotton, founder of Boston, Massachusetts. As a friend of his prayed for the dying Cotton to be given more grace, Cotton interrupted him, "He has done it already, brother," and went to heaven.

We can probably never be reminded enough that we are going to die one day and enter one of two eternal destinies—heaven or hell. I have also heard horrific stories of people who were lost and dying, which I will not go into now. Peter makes it clear that those who have followed the Lord with all their hearts will have a "rich welcome" when they pass away from this world (2 Peter 1:11).

Only Enoch had gone to heaven without dying (see Genesis 5:24; Hebrews 11:5). Now Elijah was to be the second—and what a homegoing it was! No story can match this one, although the homegoing of Stephen comes close. Just before Stephen died, he saw Jesus standing at the right hand of God (Acts 7:56). Why was Jesus standing since the Scriptures say He "sat down" at the right hand of God? Perhaps He stood "to welcome the first martyr home," as Mrs. Martyn Lloyd-Jones used to say to me. As for Dr. Lloyd-Jones, he wrote a note to me a few days before he went to heaven: "Don't pray for my healing. Pray I will be ready for the glory."

We may speculate as to what Elijah and Elisha talked about on those walks to Bethel, to Jericho and to the Jordan River. What must Elijah have been thinking, knowing he was going home that day? How would you feel if you knew you were going to die today? Would you be asking, "What will it be like—seeing Jesus?" "Will I really be reunited with my loved ones?" "Will I truly get to see people like Abraham, Moses and Paul?"

I know what Elisha was thinking: How could he get Elijah's mantle? When Elijah asked him, "What can I do for you before I am taken from you?" Elisha was ready: "Let me inherit a double portion of your spirit." He had thought it through, hoping Elijah would ask what he did.

I am not entirely sure that Elijah was thrilled with this request, although I doubt he was surprised. He knew Elisha pretty well by now. But for Elisha to get a *double portion* of Elijah's spirit? A fairly cheeky request! That would suggest that Elisha would be greater than Elijah—twice as great perhaps. We have seen in this book that Elijah wanted to be the best of all; now comes his successor who wants to have double the anointing that Elijah had.

"You have asked a difficult thing," Elijah responded. Difficult? Why? For whom? For God? Surely not. It would be difficult for Elijah. Then he relented—on one condition: "If you see me when I am taken from you, it will be yours. Otherwise not." I can safely tell you that Elisha was in Elijah's face from that moment, being careful not to look up, down or sideways—not even daring to sneeze.

They walked along, talking with what must have been both a nervous and excited expectancy for both of them. Much of the day had passed by. They had traveled so much already, it could be only a few moments—perhaps seconds—away.

Suddenly, a chariot of fire and horses of fire appeared! Elijah was separated from Elisha and went up in a whirlwind. Elisha *saw this* and cried out, "My father! My father! The chariots and horsemen of Israel." Then it was over. Elisha saw Elijah no more. He took hold of his own clothes and tore them apart. He may have panicked, or feared he had missed it. By this I mean we could argue that Elisha did not see Elijah himself but "saw this"—meaning the chariots and horsemen.

The English Standard Version says that Elisha "saw it." Not "him," but "it," *possibly* meaning the sight of the chariot of fire, the horses of fire and the whirlwind. The Living Bible says he "saw it." The Holman Apologetics Study Bible says that Elisha "watched." To be honest, this leaves a doubt whether or not Elisha saw Elijah himself as it happened. It comes down to one thing: What did *God* intend that Elisha see? Whether or not the various translations use *this* or *it* to refer to the spectacular sight as a whole rather than Elijah himself, I do not know.

There was, however, a very satisfying token that Elisha's request was granted. Elijah's cloak had fallen, and Elisha picked it up. This was a very good sign, indeed, that Elijah's mantle was passed on. I assume this meant equally that a double portion of Elijah's spirit was granted.

> Then he took the cloak that had fallen from him and struck the water with it. "Where now is the LORD, the God of Elijah?" he asked. When he struck the water, it divided to the right and to the left, and he crossed over.
>
> 2 Kings 2:14

Elijah was gone. Out of sight. In heaven. Elisha now held Elijah's mantle in his hands. He stood at the edge of the Jordan River where he had been with Elijah moments before. He asked the question, "Where now is the Lord, the God of Elijah?" As he struck the water with Elijah's mantle, the water divided to the right and to the left. He crossed over, presumably on dry ground as the two had done earlier. In any case, Elijah's mantle had been passed on to Elisha. This must have been God's plan all along; after all, it was God who led Elijah to Elisha in the first place.

One thing is for certain: Elijah was now at home. Home. "Our citizenship is in heaven," said Paul, who was a Roman citizen (see Philippians 3:20; Acts 22:28). I asked Jackie Pullinger, the legendary Christian leader in Hong Kong, "Where is home for you?" She replied by pointing her finger upward, then said: "And I really do mean that."

As I grew up in Ashland, Kentucky, I was in a quartet in my old church. We called ourselves the King David Quartet. We often sang a song that said, "This world is not my home, I'm just a-passin' through." We read in the book of Hebrews:

> Just as man is destined to die once, and after that to face judgment, so Christ was sacrificed once to take away the sins of many people; and he will appear a second time, not to bear sin, but to bring salvation to those who are waiting for him.
>
> Hebrews 9:27–28

If we are all destined to die once, how come Elijah was taken to heaven without dying? I assume he was in the category of Enoch who did not see death (Hebrews 11:5). Enoch and Elijah are exceptions, but you might be the exception, too, if you are saved and alive when Jesus comes again.

This much is sure: You and I are going to die, unless we happen to be alive when Jesus comes a second time. For most of my life I have thought I would be alive when He comes. I think most Christians hope for this. Even so, I am prepared now to die, and I want to die well.

One day there will be the sound of a trumpet that will be heard around the world all at once. "The trumpet will sound, the dead will be raised imperishable, and we will be changed" (1 Corinthians 15:52). "For the Lord himself will come down from heaven, with a loud command, with the voice of the archangel and with the trumpet call of God, and the dead in Christ will rise first" (1 Thessalonians 4:16). The dead in Christ means you and me if we die before Jesus comes. If we are still alive when He comes, then we will be "caught up" with those who died, soaring "in the clouds to meet the Lord in the air" (verse 17).

Elijah's translation was an example of being taken to heaven without dying. It was a spectacular sight, but the sight of believers being raised from the dead and taken up along with the saved who are still living will be far more spectacular. The chariot and horses of fire will seem as nothing compared to the sound of the voice of the archangel, the trump of God, countless millions being resurrected from the dead and millions more being "taken up in the clouds to meet the Lord in the air." The thought of this thrills me no end. We are in a win-win situation: If we die, we will be raised up; if we are alive when He comes we will be caught up.

Question: Are you ready for that day to come? Do you know for sure that if you die today you will go to heaven? Suppose you were standing before God (and you will) and He were to ask you (and He might), "Why should I let you into My heaven?" What would you say? It is the most important question that can be put to you. If you do not know for sure, please pray this prayer from your heart—now:

Lord Jesus Christ, I need You. I want You. I am sorry for my sins. Wash my sins away by Your blood. I know I cannot save myself. I transfer all trust in good works to Your death on the cross. I welcome Your Holy Spirit. As best as I know how, I give You my life. Amen.

If you meant that prayer with all your heart, you are as saved as Elijah. And one day you will be given a "Welcome Home" reception. The bands may not play for you here below. You may have no profile. You may be the loneliest person on earth. You may have suffered indescribable pain. You may have been rejected, disenfranchised and overlooked. You are not home yet. "I consider that our present sufferings are not worth comparing with the glory that will be revealed in us" (Romans 8:18). One day you will be "At Home." The glory will be worth waiting for.

21

In Conclusion: Elijah's Legacy

Elijah left his mark on biblical history. He came in from out of the blue, then went out in a blaze of glory like no other figure before or since. We know so little about him. Presumably he was unmarried and had no children. Apparently Elisha, too, was unmarried, but had no successor.

Whether Elisha received a "double portion" or merely continued on with Elijah's mantle is something you may want to query. Elisha certainly kept up what Elijah started, with miracles and speaking into people's lives. The best indication of his receiving a "double portion" is that the Bible records Elisha performing twice as many miracles as Elijah did. Still, he never quite achieved the spectacular authority of Elijah on Mount Carmel. Nor did he go out in a blaze of glory. Plus, it is Elijah not Elisha who is often referred to later on. Indeed, Elisha is mentioned only once in the Old Testament after his death, when a man was raised from the dead by touching his bones (see 2 Kings 13:21).

The company of the prophets from Jericho saw Elisha part the waters of the Jordan River with Elijah's mantle. They said, "The spirit of Elijah is resting on Elisha" (2 Kings 2:15). They then bowed to the ground before Elisha. When these prophets wanted to search for Elijah's body, Elisha told them not to try this. They went ahead anyway—and failed. Elisha said to them, "Didn't I tell you not to go?" (2 Kings 2:18). Elijah was never seen again—that is, until he appeared with Moses when Jesus was transfigured before His disciples (see Matthew 17:3).

Elisha continued in an "Elijah style" of ministry. He purified the water near Jericho that had been bad to drink. "The water has remained wholesome to this day," says Scripture (2 Kings 2:22). If the water known in Jericho today as "Elisha's spring" is indeed the same spring as recorded in the biblical record, I can testify to its sweetness. It is available for anybody to taste. Elisha's next miracle is not a happy one: He called down a curse on some young men who scoffed at his being bald-headed, whereupon two bears came out of the woods and mauled 42 of the youths (see 2 Kings 2:23–24).

The miracle of the widow's oil (which kept flowing until all of her jars were filled) is similar to Elijah's looking after the widow of Zarephath (see 2 Kings 4:1–7). He raised the Shunammite's son from the dead, reminding us of what Elijah had done with the son of the widow of Zarephath (see 2 Kings 4:8–37). He cured a pot of stew after it was discovered that there was "death in the pot" (see 2 Kings 4:38–42). He fed a hundred men with only twenty loaves of barley bread (see 2 Kings 4:43–44).

He healed Naaman the leper by telling him to dip seven times in the Jordan River (see 2 Kings 5:1–14). Because of the dishonesty of his servant Gehazi, Elisha caused him to be inflicted with leprosy (see 2 Kings 5:19–27). Elisha caused an iron axhead to float (see 2 Kings 6:1–7). When surrounded by enemy Arameans, he asked God to open the eyes of his servant to the angelic host around, stating that "those who are with us are more than those who are with them" (2 Kings 6:16). He then asked God to blind the enemy, and he led them to Samaria (verses 18–20).

During a great famine in Samaria, Elisha prophesied that within a day "a seah of flour will sell for a shekel and two seahs of barley for a shekel at the gate of Samaria" (2 Kings 7:1)—a word that seemed utterly absurd. It was fulfilled in a manner no one would have remotely suspected (see verses 1–20). In an astonishing act of providence the aforementioned Shunammite widow had her land restored at the moment Elijah's servant Gehazi was telling the king about her (see 2 Kings 8:1–6). He prophesied the death of Ben-Hadad, king of Aram, stating that he would be succeeded by Hazael (see 2 Kings 8:7–15).

Elisha dispatched a young man from the company of the prophets to anoint Jehu as king, which led to the deaths of Joram, Ahaziah and Jezebel—and brought Elijah back into the scenario.

> They went back and told Jehu, who said, "This is the word of the LORD that he spoke through his servant Elijah the Tish-bite: On the plot of ground at Jezreel [which had belonged to Naboth] dogs will devour Jezebel's flesh. Jezebel's body will be like refuse on the ground in the plot at Jezreel, so that no one will be able to say, 'This is Jezebel.'"
>
> 2 Kings 9:36–37

Elisha's final appearance came during the illness that took his life. First, as Elisha was dying, Jehoash, king of Israel, went to see him and wept over him, crying, "My father! My father! . . . The chariots and horsemen of Israel!" (2 Kings 13:14). Perhaps the king thought that Elisha, like Elijah, would be taken to heaven in a whirlwind. That did not happen, but Elisha did have a word for the king—his final word, in fact—that the king, when given the opportunity, should have symbolically struck his arrow on the floor more than three times, as now he would only defeat Aram three times rather than completely destroy it (see 2 Kings 13:17–19).

Elisha died and was buried (see 2 Kings 13:20). As I mentioned earlier, a man's body thrown into Elisha's tomb resulted in the man being raised from the dead (see 2 Kings 13:21). Extraordinary though Elisha's miraculous prophetic ministry was, he is not mentioned again in the Old Testament. In the New Testament, Jesus referred to him once (see Luke 4:27).

Elijah's name, however, appears several times in Scripture. The Old Testament closes with Malachi the prophet saying,

"See, I will send you the prophet Elijah before that great and dreadful day of the LORD comes. He will turn the hearts of the fathers to their children, and the hearts of the children to their fathers; or else I will come and strike the land with a curse."

Malachi 4:5–6

In the New Testament, as I noted earlier, when Gabriel the angel announced the birth of John the Baptist to Zechariah, he forecast that "he will go on before the Lord, in the spirit and power of Elijah, to turn the hearts of the fathers to their children and the disobedient to the wisdom of the righteous—to make ready a people prepared for the Lord" (Luke 1:17).

Whereas Elisha was mentioned by Jesus, it was Elijah whom everyone thought about. When John the Baptist preached in the desert, Jews from Jerusalem wanted to know who he was, and they asked, "Are you Elijah?" (John 1:21). He said He was not.

In one of Jesus' first statements after His claim to be the Anointed One, spoken of in Isaiah 61:1 (see Luke 4:18–21), He referred to Elijah going to the widow of Zarephath (Luke 4:26). King Herod, upon hearing about Jesus, feared that He was John the Baptist raised from the dead, but others said, "He [Jesus] is Elijah" (Mark 6:15). Although John the Baptist said that he himself was not Elijah, Jesus said that John was indeed "the Elijah who was to come" (Matthew 11:14).

Jesus asked His disciples, "Who do people say the Son of Man is?" They replied, "Some say John the Baptist; others say Elijah" (Matthew 16:13–14). As we saw, Elijah appeared with Moses when Jesus was transfigured (see Matthew 17:3). When Jesus was dying on the cross and cried out, "*Eloi, Eloi, lama sabachthani?*"—which means, "My God, my God, why have you forsaken me?"—some said, "He's calling Elijah." They added, "Let's see if Elijah comes to save him" (see Matthew 27:46–49).

The apostle Paul referred to Elijah's comment, "Lord, they have killed your prophets and torn down your altars; I am the only one left, and they are trying to kill me" (Romans 11:3). Then Paul quoted God's answer to him: "I have reserved for myself seven thousand who have not bowed the knee to Baal" (verse 4). James mentioned Elijah in the context of effectual fervent praying, pointing out that Elijah prayed that it might not rain and then prayed that it would rain, pointing out that Elijah was a man "just like us" (James 5:17–18).

There are no other references to Elijah unless you take the view that he is one of the two witnesses described in Revelation 11:1–12. That is, however, to delve into eschatological speculation outside the purview of this book.

Elijah was a holy man. He could not be bribed for any amount of money. He was colorful, extraordinary, ordinary, lonely and very human. I look forward to seeing him in heaven.

May God Almighty, Father, Son and Holy Spirit rest upon you—now and evermore. Amen.

Dr. R. T. Kendall was born in Ashland, Kentucky, on July 13, 1935. He has been married to Louise for more than fifty years. They have two children, a son (Robert Tillman II, married to Annette) and a daughter (Melissa), and one grandson (Tobias Robert Stephen).

R. T. is a graduate of Trevecca Nazarene University (A.B.), Southern Baptist Theological Seminary (M.Div.), the University of Louisville (M.A.) and Oxford University (D.Phil. *Oxon.*). His doctoral thesis was published by Oxford University Press under the title *Calvin and English Calvinism to 1647*. He was awarded the D.D. by Trevecca Nazarene University in 2008.

Before he and his family went to England, R. T. pastored churches in Palmer, Tennessee; Carlisle, Ohio; Fort Lauderdale, Florida; and Salem, Indiana. He was pastor of Calvary Baptist Church in Lower Heyford, Oxfordshire, England (paralleling his three years at Oxford). He became the minister of Westminster Chapel on February 1, 1977, and was there for exactly 25 years, succeeding G. Campbell Morgan and D. Martyn Lloyd-Jones. He retired on February 1, 2002. His wrote about his 25 years at Westminster Chapel in his book *In Pursuit of His Glory*.

Shortly after Dr. Kendall's "retirement," he became involved in the Alexandria Peace Process, founded by Lord

Carey, former Archbishop of Canterbury, and Canon Andrew White, the archbishop's envoy to the Middle East. From this came a special relationship with the late Yasser Arafat, president of the Palestinian National Authority, and Rabbi David Rosen, Israel's most distinguished orthodox Jewish rabbi. R. T. and David wrote a book together, *The Christian and the Pharisee*.

Dr. Kendall is the author of more than fifty books, including *Total Forgiveness*, *The Anointing*, *Sensitivity of the Spirit*, *The Parables of Jesus*, *God Meant It for Good* and *Did You Think to Pray?* He has an international ministry and spends his time preaching and writing. He and Louise currently live on Hickory Lake in Hendersonville, Tennessee, where he fishes occasionally.